THE 5-MINUTE
Japanese Noodles
COOKBOOK

Etsuko Ichise

TUTTLE Publishing

Tokyo | Rutland, Vermont | Singapore

CONTENTS

Savory Salted Noodles

Similar Noodle Dishes from Other Parts of Asia!

Miso Flavored Noodles

Similar Noodle Dishes from Other Parts of Asia!

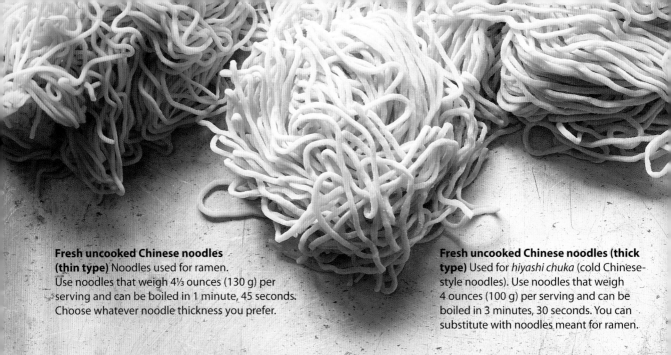

Fresh uncooked Chinese noodles (thin type) Noodles used for ramen. Use noodles that weigh 4⅓ ounces (130 g) per serving and can be boiled in 1 minute, 45 seconds. Choose whatever noodle thickness you prefer.

Fresh uncooked Chinese noodles (thick type) Used for *hiyashi chuka* (cold Chinese-style noodles). Use noodles that weigh 4 ounces (100 g) per serving and can be boiled in 3 minutes, 30 seconds. You can substitute with noodles meant for ramen.

Why I Wrote This Book

Just toss a fried egg and some crunchy tempura batter bits on top of cooked noodles … you might think, "is that all there is to it?" But it's delicious, so that's all that matters! In our household, when we're in a hurry, we make something like "Poached Egg Soba with Tempura Bits" (page 14). In the summer, we often eat *hiyashi chuka* (cold Ramen with Bacon & Lettuce—page 34). The ingredients and toppings can be any meats or vegetables you have in the fridge. These are not elaborate meals—but they aren't shortcuts either. In this book, I present a large variety of simple and delicious noodle dishes that are reminiscent of the stir-fried noodles that my family ate together for lunch on Saturdays when I was a child.

Instant noodles are convenient and delicious, but eating them too often raises health concerns. This book was inspired by the idea that delicious noodle dishes can be cooked in the same amount of time that it takes to prepare instant

Frozen soba noodles
Use noodles that weigh 6 ounces (175 g) per serving that can be boiled in 1 minute. You can also cook them in the microwave. I recommend using frozen soba noodles, which are very convenient, but you can use dried soba noodles too, of course.

Frozen udon noodles
Use frozen udon noodles that weigh 6 ounces (175 g) per serving and are boiled for 1 minute. You can also cook them in the microwave. Use your favorite type of udon noodles, such as Sanuki or Inaniwa.

noodles. With remote work becoming more popular, a lot of people are facing the challenge of deciding what to make for lunch every day. This collection of recipes is a perfect fit for people in this situation. Although only basic ingredients are used, I have included a wide range of variations so you can enjoy many different flavors. If your udon or somen noodle dishes always seem to taste the same, this book solves your problem! To help you prepare these recipes as quickly as possible, I call for using canned foods, ingredients that are close at hand, and minimum effort.

The book also provides an array of ingredient substitution options. Feel free to mix and match to use up leftover ingredients in your refrigerator. If you want to change things up a bit, refer to the "Extra" toppings suggestions. You can enjoy the same recipe with a brand new spin!

Noodles can be delicious however they're prepared! Enjoy these simple and tasty noodle dishes.

—Etsuko Ichise

Thin ramen noodles
Use pre-steamed Chinese noodles, 5 ounces (150 g) per serving, heated in the microwave for 30 seconds and loosened up before using. Some recipes call for using these noodles as-is.

Somen noodles
Use a 2-ounce (50-g) bundle of dried noodles with a boiling time of 1 minute, 30 seconds to 2 minutes. Hiyamugi noodles can be used instead.

WHEN YOU COOK WITH BASIC SEASONINGS…

① You can make the recipes right away!
Because no special seasonings are needed, you can make these recipes quickly and easily with whatever you have on hand. But the variations are endless. You can create a multitude of flavors with the same seasonings, and you will never get bored!

② You can make the meal as wholesome as you like!
Because the recipes only use a basic set of seasonings, they are lower in sodium and calories than instant noodles. In addition, because you are using seasonings that you are familiar with, you know exactly what is going into your food.

③ You do not need storebought noodle soup base (*mentsuyu*)!
Mentsuyu, or "noodle sauce," is commercially prepared sauce for making noodles that is very popular as a seasoning in Japan. But because the recipes in this book are made by combining only basic seasonings, you don't even need mentsuyu. Mentsuyu is convenient to have handy, but it does not keep very long and tends to make everything taste the same. However, you can enjoy a variety of flavors with the seasonings you have on hand using the recipes in this book.

About the Eight Basic Seasonings in This Book

This book uses eight "basic seasonings" that most Japanese households have on hand. All of these ingredients can be purchased in Japanese grocery stores and many general Asian grocery stores, and some are easily available in regular supermarkets. Each recipe is designed to bring out a variety of flavors by adding just a little bit of spiciness or sweetness with seasonings. You do not have to buy expensive or exotic seasonings—just use the ones you have on hand.

Black and white pepper I prefer to use black and white pepper that's been freshly ground in a pepper mill, but you can use pre-ground pepper instead.

Mirin Use real mirin (sweet rice wine for cooking)—any brand that you prefer is fine. The product sold as "mirin seasoning" has an entirely different flavor.

Miso I use Shinshu miso (with a sodium content at around 12%), but use the miso that you prefer. Each brand of miso has a different flavor, so adjust the amount to taste.

Salt I use refined salt. You can use kosher salt or pink salt instead, but they are less salty than refined salt, so you'll need to adjust the amounts used. In addition, if you substitute an ingredient specified in the ingredient lists with the "substitute" (**or ▶**) indicator, the flavor may change a bit, so please adjust the amount of salt used accordingly.

Saké You can go for a cheap variety, but use a saké intended for drinking rather than a cooking saké (which is overly salty and sweet).

Soy Sauce I use organic soy sauce, but you can use your favorite variety.

Sugar I use white caster sugar, but cane sugar can be used instead. The sugar that you normally use is fine.

Vinegar Use rice vinegar. White vinegar is too acidic and too strong.

Dashi Soup Stock

When "dashi" is specified in an ingredient list, I am calling for dashi soup stock that is made with kombu seaweed and bonito flakes. You can use premade dashi stock granules, but if you have the time, I suggest making your own dashi from scratch (see below). For Chinese-style and Western-style recipes, I use soup powders or granules.

Chinese chicken soup stock granules Soup stock that is made with a chicken base. This is used mainly in Chinese-style dishes. I use a brand that does not include monosodium glutamate.

Bonito flakes When making dashi, don't use the type of bonito flakes that are finely flaked and come in tiny packets. Use the ones that have large, thin flakes and come in big bags.

Kombu seaweed There are different varieties of kombu seaweed, such as Rishiri kombu or Hidaka kombu. You can use whatever variety you have on hand.

Consommé granules This is soup stock that has the concentrated flavors of meats and aromatic vegetables. If you are using the cube type, 2 teaspoons of granules equals 1 cube.

How to Make Dashi Stock

1. Lightly wipe off any residue from the surface of one to two 4 x 2.5-inch (10 x 5-cm) pieces of kombu seaweed using a thick paper towel that's been moistened and firmly wrung out. Put the kombu seaweed in a pan, add 5 cups (1.2 liters) of water, and leave to soak for about 30 minutes.
2. Heat the pan over low heat. When small bubbles form, remove the seaweed.
3. Turn the heat up to high, and just as the water comes to a boil, add ⅔ oz (20 g) of bonito flakes and give them a stir to spread them out in the pan. Turn the heat down to low immediately and simmer for 1 minute. Turn off the heat, and let stand until the bonito flakes have sunk to the bottom.
4. Pass the liquid through a colander lined with a paper towel. Discard the solids.

This recipe makes about 4¼ cups (1 liter) of dashi.
To store: allow it to cool, and then transfer it to a storage container and refrigerate it for up to 3 days, or freeze it for up to 3 weeks.

Kombu Seaweed

**Bonito Flakes
(*Katsuobushi*)**

Controlling Spiciness

In this book, in addition to the basic seasonings, I call for red chili peppers, Chinese chili paste (*dou-banjiang*), sesame chili oil (*la-yu*) and ground chili pepper to add some heat. If you don't like spicy food, or are cooking for children, simply reduce or eliminate the chili pepper-based ingredients.

About Other Ingredients

• Olive oil, sesame oil and other oils are also used as seasonings and sauces for mixed noodles and other dishes.

• Soy milk used for soups and sauces should be unsweetened, but sweetened soy milk can be used in a pinch. I've also used regular cow's milk.

How to Use This Book

• All amounts are for 2 servings.
• Cooking times are approximate. All recipes are designed to take around 5 minutes to complete from the time you start cooking the noodles and other ingredients. I have not included the prep time for cutting vegetables and so on in the cooking time.
• The amounts specified for vegetables and so on include the skins and seeds. The steps for washing and peeling them have been omitted.
• Organic, unwaxed lemons are used.
• A 600-watt microwave oven is used. If your microwave oven's wattage differs, please adjust the cooking times.
• 1 tablespoon is 15 ml, 1 teaspoon is 5 ml, and a pinch is pinched with 3 fingers.

Consommé Granules

Chinese Chicken Soup Stock (Granules)

How to Drain Noodles

Simply draining noodles by shaking them in a colander is actually not enough. Press on them firmly with your hands to get the water out completely. If the noodles are still very wet, their texture will not be ideal, and the flavors will become dissipated, so drain them very well.

1. Put the boiled noodles in a colander, and pour cold running water over them immediately.
2. When the noodles have cooled down, massage them with your hands to remove the surface sliminess as you continue to run cold water over them.
3. When the noodles are cool, stop running cold water over them, and press the noodles firmly into the colander to remove the excess water.

Time-saving Tips

In this book, the recipes are all designed to be completed in about 5 minutes from the time you start to cook. The following ingredients and tools are useful, so it's a good idea to have them on hand.

Tip 1

Use meats that cook quickly
If you use ground meat or thinly cut meat meant for shabu shabu (available in Asian grocery stores), they cook almost immediately, and you can save a ton of time. If you are using a large piece of meat such as a whole chicken thigh, cut it into small pieces so that it cooks quickly.

Tip 2

Convenient, make-ahead steamed chicken
This is a method for making steamed chicken that can be prepared easily in the microwave. If you make it in advance when you have the opportunity, it will be available at a moment's notice, saving the time needed to cook the meat. This keeps for about 4 days in the refrigerator. You can also substitute this with 4 ounces (100 g) of chicken tenderloins sprinkled with a pinch of salt and ½ tablespoon saké and microwaved for 1 minute 40 seconds.

1. Place about 8 ounces (250 g) of boneless chicken breast with its skin on in a microwave-safe container with the skin-side facing down. Rub ¼ teaspoon salt on the side without skin and leave at room temperature for about 15 minutes.
2. Sprinkle with 1 tablespoon of saké, and cover the chicken loosely with cling wrap; microwave for about 2 minutes. Turn the chicken breast over—repositioning the cling wrap to cover again—and microwave for another 2 minutes or so. Leave with the cling wrap in place to continue cooking with residual heat for about 15 more minutes as it cools down.
3. Wrap tightly with cling wrap, and place in a storage container—including the cooking juices—with the skin side facing up, and secure the lid.
  • Use ½ chicken breast per 2 servings of noodles.
  • Use a chicken breast that is less than 1¼-inch (3-cm) thick.

Tip 3

Shorten cooking times by using canned and prepared foods

Precooked sausages, bacon, canned tuna and canned mackerel are already cooked, so they shorten the preparation time drastically. In addition, they each have their own distinct umami to add even more delicious flavor to the noodles.

Tip 4

Handy ingredients that lend instant flavors

Napa cabbage kimchi, *umeboshi* (salt-preserved *ume* fruit), *shio kombu* (salt-preserved kombu seaweed) and red shiso-leaf *furikake* (seasoned seaweed sprinkles) and other ingredients that already have bold flavors of their own can be used in small quantities to nail down the flavor, thus cutting down on cooking time. You can use these ingredients to add an instant punch of complexity and flavor, so they are invaluable.

Tip 5

Steam-cooking in a skillet is simple and saves on clean up

Some *yakisoba* (stir-fried noodle) dishes, such as the "Ground Meat & Bell Pepper Ramen" on page 30, use a cooking method where all the ingredients are put into a skillet, then simply covered with a lid and steam-cooked. This is a method that makes it easy to cook as well as clean up, which saves time.

SOY SAUCE
FLAVORED
NOODLES

Simple Kama-age Udon

Kama-age udon is an udon dish with eggs and udon noodles. It is the ultimate quick and simple way to prepare udon. All you need to do is boil the noodles, add the toppings and you're done! It is simple, but the combination is *so* delicious. Add any toppings that you like!

2 SERVINGS

2 servings frozen udon noodles **or** 2 servings frozen soba noodles
2 raw egg yolks* **or** 2 hot-spring poached eggs (see next page)
Bonito flakes, finely minced green onions (scallions), shredded nori seaweed, to taste
2 tablespoons soy sauce

*Use very fresh eggs or pasteurized eggs

1. Bring plenty of water to a boil in a pan, cook the udon noodles according to the package instructions, and drain into a colander.
2. Arrange the udon noodles in serving bowls, top with the egg yolks, bonito flakes, minced green onions and shredded nori seaweed and drizzle with the soy sauce.

Extra

This is delicious topped with thinly sliced steamed chicken (page 10) too!

Extra

This is delicious topped with some coarsely ground chili pepper or *shichimi togarashi* (seven-ingredient chili pepper condiment)!

Poached Egg Soba with Tempura Bits

Simply adding tempura batter bits to noodles makes them a lot more satisfying! Adding some spice is wonderful too.

2 SERVINGS

2 servings frozen soba noodles
or 2 servings frozen udon noodles
6 tablespoons tempura batter bits (see note)
2 hot-spring poached eggs *or* 2 fresh or pasteurized raw egg yolks
Radish sprouts, roots trimmed, to taste
2 tablespoons soy sauce

1. Bring plenty of water to a boil in a pan, boil the soba noodles according to the package instructions, and drain into a colander.
2. Arrange the soba noodles in serving bowls, top with the tempura batter bits, hot-spring poached eggs and radish sprouts, and drizzle with soy sauce.

How to make hot-spring poached eggs *(onsen tamago)*
Hot-spring eggs are soft-poached in their shell. They have runny whites as well as runny yolks. Be sure to use very fresh or pasteurized eggs, because the eggs are only partially cooked.

Bring 3⅓ cups (800 ml) of water to a boil in a small pan, about 7 inches (18 cm) in diameter. Take the pan off the heat. Add ⅔ cup (150 ml) of cold water and the eggs straight out of the fridge. Cover the pan with a lid and set aside for 15 minutes. Crack the eggs carefully onto the noodles.

Note: Tempura batter bits are small pieces of batter left over after making tempura. They are sold in bags and called *tenkasu* or *agetama*. You can also make your own by keeping the bits of tempura batter left over after making tempura and freezing them for later use.

Extra
This is delicious topped with mayonnaise to finish!

Ramen Topped with Fried Egg, Sausage & Greens

Hiyashi chuka is a chilled noodle dish made with Chinese noodles that was invented in Japan. This version is topped with a cute fried egg, and is easy and healthy.

2 SERVINGS

2 servings fresh uncooked Chinese noodles (thick type) **or** 2 servings frozen udon noodles
1 tablespoon oil
2 eggs
Salt and coarse freshly ground black pepper, to taste
3 small Vienna sausages or 1 frankfurter, sliced thinly diagonally **or** 3 slices bacon, cut into 1-in (2.5-cm) pieces
1⅓ oz (40 g) baby greens **or** 2 to 3 lettuce leaves, torn into bite-size pieces

A ingredients—mix together:
2 tablespoons soy sauce
2 tablespoons rice vinegar
2 tablespoons water
1 tablespoon sugar
1 tablespoon sesame oil

1. Bring plenty of water to a boil in a pan and cook the Chinese noodles according to the package instructions. Drain into a colander, rinse with cold running water, and drain well.
2. Heat up a skillet with the oil over medium-high heat. Break in the eggs and sprinkle with salt and black pepper. Cook to your desired degree of doneness. Place the sliced sausage in the empty space in the skillet and stir-fry.
3. Arrange the Chinese noodles on serving plates, top with the baby greens, sausage and fried eggs, and drizzle with the combined A ingredients.

Lemony Noodles with Pork & Lettuce

Although this is substantial because of the meat, it has a refreshing finish due to the addition of lemon. Since it has plenty of vegetables in it, you can eat this dish like a salad.

2 SERVINGS

4 oz (100 g) very thinly cut pork for shabu shabu *or* ½ portion make-ahead steamed chicken (see page 10), thinly sliced

2 servings fresh uncooked Chinese noodles (thick type) *or* 2 servings frozen udon noodles

4 leaves loose-leaf lettuce (about 2 oz / 50 g) *or* 2 to 3 lettuce leaves *or* the equivalent amount of baby lettuce leaves, **torn into bite-size pieces**

⅛ red onion, sliced thinly *or* ⅛ regular onion, sliced thinly

Lemon wedges, for serving

A ingredients:
3 tablespoons olive oil
2 tablespoons soy sauce
½ tablespoon fresh lemon juice

Extra

Try topping this with bite-size pieces of Camembert or mozzarella cheese!

1. Bring plenty of water to a boil in a pan and turn the heat down to low. Add the pork and cook it until it changes color. Drain in a colander until cooled. Bring the water in the pan back to a boil, and boil the Chinese noodles according to the package instructions. Drain into a colander, rinse with cold running water, and drain well.
2. Put the A ingredients in a bowl and mix well. Add the Chinese noodles, pork, lettuce and red onion, and mix.
3. Distribute onto serving plates and serve with lemon wedges. Squeeze on the lemon to eat.

Extra

Great topped with some roasted white sesame seeds!

Somen with Pork, Salted Plum & Grated Cucumber

The grated cucumber with umeboshi preserved plum has a very refreshing taste.

2 SERVINGS

4 oz (100 g) very thinly cut pork for shabu shabu

3 bundles (5 oz / 150 g) dried somen noodles **or** 2 servings frozen udon noodles

2 baby cucumbers, grated

2 *umeboshi* (salt preserved *ume* fruit), about 1 oz (30 g)

A ingredients—mix together:

1 cup (250 ml) chilled dashi stock (see page 8)

1 tablespoon soy sauce

½ teaspoon sugar

½ teaspoon salt

1. Bring plenty of water to a boil in a pan and turn the heat down to low. Add the pork and cook it until it changes color. Drain in a colander until cooled. Bring the water in the pan back to a boil, and cook the somen noodles according to the package instructions. Drain into a colander, rinse with cold running water, and drain well.

2. Arrange the somen noodles in containers, top with the pork, cucumber and *umeboshi*, and pour the combined A ingredients over top.

Note: Use *umeboshi* that has 15% or less salt content. Adjust the amount of salt used depending on how salty the *umeboshi* is.

Extra

If you add coarsely ground black pepper or chili pepper to finish, the flavors will really come together!

Pork & Cabbage Stir-Fried Somen

Champuru is a traditional stir-fried vegetable dish from Okinawa. Simply adding soy sauce and sesame oil adds amazing depth to the flavor!

2 SERVINGS

3 bundles (5 oz / 150 g) dried somen noodles **or** 2 servings frozen udon noodles
½ tablespoon sesame oil
1 teaspoon oil
5 oz (150 g) roughly chopped pork, sprinkled with salt and freshly ground black pepper
2 cabbage leaves (approx. 3½ oz / 85 g) **or** 1–2 napa cabbage leaves, cut into 3-in (7.5-cm) long thin strips
½ onion, thinly sliced **or** 3½ oz (85 g) mushrooms of your choice, cut into bite-size pieces

A ingredients:
2 tablespoons soy sauce
Small pinch of freshly ground black pepper

1. Bring plenty of water to a boil in a pan and cook the somen noodles according to the package instructions. Drain into a colander, rinse with cold running water, and drain well. Mix with the sesame oil.
2. Heat up the oil in a skillet over medium heat, and stir-fry the pork. When the meat changes color, add the cabbage and onion and continue stir-frying. When the vegetables are wilted, add the somen noodles and the A ingredients and stir-fry quickly.

Pork, Kimchi & Soy Milk Udon

By using commercially prepared kimchi, you can make a substantial noodle meal with ease! The richness of the soy milk is so delicious. This is a healthy noodle dish that will give you lots of energy!

2 SERVINGS

2 servings frozen udon noodles **or** 3 bundles dried somen noodles
½ tablespoon oil
5 oz (150 g) roughly chopped pork **or** 5 oz (150 g) thinly sliced pork belly (cut into 2-in / 5-cm pieces)
8 shishito peppers with a slit cut into each **or** 2 small bell or padron peppers, sliced *or* ½ large bell pepper, sliced
3 oz (75 g) napa cabbage kimchi, chopped
1 teaspoon soy sauce
La-yu chili oil, to taste

A ingredients—mix together:
1 cup (250 ml) soy milk
1 tablespoon soy sauce

Extra

This is delicious sprinkled with ground white sesame seeds or chili pepper threads!

1. Bring plenty of water to a boil in a pan and boil the udon noodles according to the package instructions. Drain into a colander, rinse with cold running water, and drain well.
2. Heat up the oil in a skillet over medium heat, add the pork and shishito peppers, and stir-fry. When the pork changes color, add the kimchi and soy sauce, and stir-fry quickly.
3. Arrange the udon noodles on serving plates, and top with the step-2 ingredients. Pour on the combined A ingredients, and drizzle with some la-yu chili oil.

Extra

Try adding cut up mushrooms or burdock root in step 1!

Udon with Pork Belly & Leek Broth

The pork belly spreads richness in the dipping sauce for a deeply flavored finish.

2 SERVINGS

4 oz (100 g) thinly cut pork belly, cut into 1-in (2.5-cm) pieces **or** 4 oz (100 g) roughly chopped pork

1 **Asian leek** **or** 2 large green onions (scallions) *or* ½ onion, **thinly sliced diagonally**

2 **servings frozen udon noodles** **or** 2 servings frozen soba noodles

Coarsely ground chili pepper, to taste

A ingredients:

1¼ **cups (300 ml) dashi stock** (see page 8)

2 **tablespoons soy sauce**

2 **tablespoons mirin**

1. Put the A ingredients in a pan and mix. Bring to a boil over high heat, add the pork and leek, and simmer over medium heat for about 2 minutes.

2. In a separate pan, bring plenty of water to a boil, cook the udon noodles according to the package instructions, and drain into a colander. Rinse with cold running water, and drain well.

3. Arrange the udon in bowls. Put the step-1 ingredients in separate bowls, sprinkle with coarsely ground chili pepper, and serve with the udon. Dip the udon noodles in the sauce to eat.

Extra
Sprinkle on some coarsely ground black pepper to finish, or add a little more vinegar to make this even tastier!

Hot & Sour Noodle Soup with Pork & Mushrooms

The umami of the pork belly and mushrooms is delicious! Adjust the sourness and spiciness with the vinegar and la-yu chili oil.

2 SERVINGS

4 oz (100 g) thinly sliced pork belly, cut into ⅓-in (1-cm) pieces
4 oz (100 g) enoki mushrooms **or** 4 oz (100 g) shimeji mushrooms, **stems separated and bases trimmed**
4 shiitake mushrooms **or** 1 king oyster mushroom, **stems removed and thinly sliced**
1 egg, beaten
1 tablespoon rice vinegar
2 servings fresh uncooked Chinese noodles (thin type)
La-yu chili oil, to taste

A ingredients:
3 cups (750 ml) water
1 tablespoon Chinese chicken soup stock granules
3 tablespoons rice vinegar
2½ tablespoons soy sauce
¼ teaspoon sesame oil

B ingredients—mix together until the starch is dissolved:
2 teaspoons potato starch or cornstarch
4 teaspoons water

1. Put the A ingredients in a pan and mix. Bring to a boil over high heat, add the pork, enoki mushrooms and shiitake mushrooms, and simmer over medium heat for about 3 minutes. Add the combined B ingredients and stir. When the soup has thickened slightly add the beaten egg and vinegar in that order, and mix quickly.
2. In a separate pan, bring plenty of water to a boil and cook the Chinese noodles according to the package instructions. Drain into a colander.
3. Arrange the Chinese noodles into bowls, add the step-1 ingredients and drizzle with la-yu chili oil.

Soba Noodles with Chicken and Greens

The refreshing flavor of raw okra is so fresh! Boiling the soba noodles and the greens together saves a lot of cooking time and effort. I also recommend adding shredded nori seaweed as a topping.

2 SERVINGS

2 servings frozen or dried soba noodles or
   2 servings frozen udon noodles *or* 3 bundles dried somen noodles
1 small bundle (about 5 oz / 150 g) *komatsuna* greens or spinach, **cut into 2-in (5-cm) pieces**
½ make-ahead steamed chicken (see page 10), thinly sliced or 4 oz (100 g) thinly sliced pork belly for shabu shabu, boiled
2 okra or 4 shishito peppers, **sliced into thin rounds**

A ingredients—mix together:
1¾ cups (425 ml) chilled dashi stock
2 tablespoons soy sauce
⅔ teaspoon salt
½ teaspoon sugar

Extra

Delicious topped with grated mountain yam or shredded nori seaweed too!

1. Bring plenty of water to a boil in a pan, and cook the soba noodles according to the package instructions. Add the cut up *komatsuna* greens 30 seconds before the noodles have finished cooking. Drain them both into a colander, rinse with cold running water, and drain well.
2. Put the step-1 ingredients into serving bowls, top with the steamed chicken and okra, and pour the A ingredients over top.

NOTE: If you are using shishito peppers instead of okra, you can just slice them thinly and use them raw.

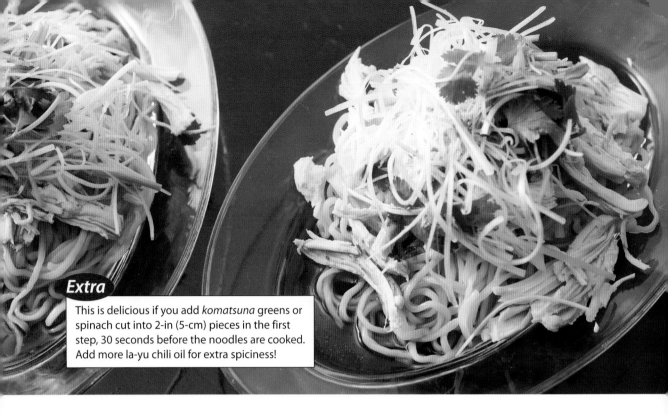

Ramen with Shredded Chicken & Leek

As long as you have make-ahead steamed chicken on hand, you can make this dish in a jiffy! The spicy flavors really whet your appetite.

2 SERVINGS

2 servings fresh uncooked Chinese noodles (thick type) **or** 3 bundles dried somen noodles

½ **Asian leek or** 1 large green onion (scallion), **cut into 2-in (5-cm) pieces, shredded, put into cold water and drained**

1 small bundle fresh coriander leaves (cilantro), cut into 1-in (2.5-cm) pieces

½ **make-ahead steamed chicken (see page 10), skin removed and cut into bite-size pieces or** 4 oz (100 g) thinly sliced pork for shabu shabu, boiled

A ingredients—mix together:
2 tablespoons soy sauce
2 tablespoons water
1 tablespoon rice vinegar
1 tablespoon sesame oil
2 teaspoons sugar
½ teaspoon la-yu chili oil
½ teaspoon doubanjiang
Grated garlic, to taste

1. Bring plenty of water to a boil in a pan and boil the Chinese noodles according to the package instructions. Drain into a colander, rinse with cold running water, and drain well.
2. Mix the leek and coriander together.
3. Arrange the noodles on serving plates, top with the steamed chicken and the step-2 ingredients, and drizzle with the combined A ingredients.

Extra

This is delicious topped with mayonnaise to finish!

Ramen with Chicken, Grated Daikon & Avocado

Avocado and grated daikon radish go together surprisingly well.

2 SERVINGS

2 chicken tenderloins, sinews removed—about 4 oz (100 g) or ½ make-ahead steamed chicken (see page 10), shredded *or* 4 oz (100 g) thinly sliced pork for shabu shabu, boiled

2 servings fresh uncooked Chinese noodles (thick type) or 2 servings frozen udon noodles

1 avocado, cut in half, pit removed, peeled and mashed roughly with a fork

7 oz (200 g) daikon radish, grated and drained in a colander or 1 small cucumber, sliced thinly and rubbed with salt

Roasted sesame seeds, to taste

A ingredients—mix together:
½ tablespoon saké
Pinch of salt

B ingredients—mix together:
2 tablespoons soy sauce
2 tablespoons sesame oil
⅔ teaspoon wasabi paste

1. Place the chicken on a microwave-safe plate. Sprinkle with the A ingredients. Cover loosely with cling wrap and microwave for about 1 minute, 40 seconds. Leave the cling wrap on to continue cooking with residual heat. Once cooled, shred the chicken into bite-size pieces.
2. Bring plenty of water to a boil in a pan and boil the Chinese noodles according to the package instructions. Drain into a colander, rinse with cold running water, and drain well.
3. Arrange the noodles on serving plates, top with the chicken, mashed avocado and grated daikon radish. Pour the B ingredients over top and sprinkle with sesame seeds.

Extra

Try adding some roasted white sesame seeds or coarsely ground chili pepper!

Noodles with Chicken, Greens & Olive-Soy Dressing

Add richness and umami to lightly flavored chicken tenderloins with olive oil and soy sauce.

2 SERVINGS

2 chicken tenderloins, sinews removed—about 4 oz (100 g) *or* ½ make-ahead steamed chicken (see page 10), shredded *or* 4 oz (100 g) thinly sliced pork for shabu shabu, boiled

3 bundles (5 oz / 150 g) dried somen noodles *or* 2 servings fresh Chinese noodles (thick type) *or* 2 servings frozen udon noodles

Small bundle *mizuna* greens, about 2 oz (50 g), cut into 1-in (2.5-cm) pieces *or* 2–3 leaves iceberg or loose-leaf lettuce, torn

Nori seaweed, to taste

A ingredients—mix together:
½ tablespoon saké
Pinch of salt

B ingredients—mix together:
2 tablespoons olive oil
2 tablespoons soy sauce

1. Place the chicken tenderloins on a microwave-safe plate and sprinkle with the A ingredients. Cover loosely with cling wrap and microwave for about 1 minute, 40 seconds. Leave with the cling wrap on to continue cooking with residual heat. When the chicken has cooled down, shred into bite-size pieces.

2. Bring plenty of water to a boil in a pan and boil the somen noodles according to the package instructions. Drain into a colander, rinse with cold running water, and drain well.

3. Put the somen noodles, chicken tenderloins and *mizuna* greens into a bowl and mix together. Arrange on serving plates, tear up the nori seaweed and put on top, drizzle with the B ingredients, and mix well to eat.

Extra

Try adding grated mountain yam at the end for a delicious variation!

Beef Sukiyaki Udon with Eggplant

The sukiyaki-style sweet and salty flavors whet your appetite irresistibly.

2 SERVINGS

5 oz (150 g) thinly sliced chopped beef `or` 5 oz (150 g) chopped pork *or* 5 oz (150 g) thinly sliced pork belly, cut into 2-in (5-cm) pieces

1 Asian eggplant, cut into half lengthwise and sliced thinly diagonally `or` 1 Asian leek, sliced thinly diagonally *or* ½ green onion (scallion), sliced thinly

2 servings frozen udon noodles `or` 3 bundles dried somen noodles

2 fresh or pasteurized egg yolks `or` 2 hot-spring poached eggs (see page 14)

Beni-shoga red pickled ginger, to taste

A ingredients—mix together:
⅔ cup (160 ml) dashi stock
3 tablespoons mirin
2½ tablespoons soy sauce
½ tablespoon sugar

1. Put the A ingredients in a skillet and mix together. Bring to a boil over medium heat, add the beef and eggplant, and simmer for about 3 minutes, turning over occasionally.
2. Bring plenty of water to a boil in a pan, cook the udon noodles according to the package instructions, and drain into a colander.
3. Arrange the udon in serving bowls, and add the step-1 ingredients. Top each bowl with an egg yolk each and red pickled ginger.

Ground Meat & Bell Pepper Ramen

Instead of the usual yakisoba sauce used for these types of stir-fried noodles, I have used soy sauce as the main seasoning! This goes with the noodles really well. Black pepper brings the flavors together, and lemon is added for a refreshing finish.

2 SERVINGS

2 servings ramen noodles
½ large red bell pepper, sliced thinly lengthwise
5 oz (150 g) ground pork **or** 5 oz (150 g) ground beef, sprinkled with 3 tablespoons mirin, 2 tablespoons soy sauce and coarse freshly ground black pepper, to taste
4 tablespoons water
Coarse freshly ground black pepper, to taste
1 lemon, cut in half

1. Place the ramen noodles in a skillet, and add the bell pepper and ground meat in individual layers in that order. Swirl in the water, cover with a lid, and steam-cook for about 4 minutes over high heat.
2. Take off the lid, and stir-fry until all the meat has changed color.
3. Arrange on serving plates, and sprinkle with coarsely ground black pepper. Serve with a lemon half on the side and squeeze it on before eating.

NOTE: I have used a 10-in (25-cm) diameter skillet. Arrange the ramen noodles in the skillet so that they overlap as little as possible.

Extra

Try adding garlic chives or thin green onions (scallions) cut into 2-in (5-cm) pieces at step 2. Adding grated cheese at the end is delicious too!

Extra

Try topping with some shredded nori seaweed!

Udon with Spicy Soboro

Soboro is a delicious blend of ground meat, tofu, eggs and seasonings. It goes well with rice as well as noodles. The spice level is controlled by the amount of doubanjiang added.

2 SERVINGS

2 servings frozen udon noodles **or**
  3 bundles dried somen noodles
7 oz (200 g) ground chicken **or**
  7 oz (200 g) ground pork, **mixed
  with 2 tablespoons soy sauce,
  2 tablespoons mirin, 1 tablespoon
  sugar and ½ teaspoon doubanjiang**
2 hot-spring poached eggs (see page
  14) **or** 2 fresh or pasteurized raw
  egg yolks
Asian leek (thinly sliced) **or** large
  green onion (scallion), **to taste**

NOTE: See page 14 for instructions
for making hot-spring poached eggs.

1. Bring plenty of water to a boil in a pan, cook the udon noodles according to the package instructions, and drain into a colander.
2. Put the ground meat in a skillet over medium heat, and stir-fry while breaking up the meat. When it changes color, add the udon noodles and continue stir-frying.
3. Arrange on serving plates, and top each with a hot-spring poached egg and the leek.

Extra

If you sprinkle on coarsely ground black pepper to finish, the flavors will really come together!

Udon with Ham, Mushrooms & Soy-Butter Sauce

This is a perfectly rich combination of flavors! You can use sausage or bacon instead of ham.

2 SERVINGS

2 servings frozen udon noodles
1 tablespoon oil
½ onion, cut into ⅓-in (1-cm) wedges
4 oz (100 g) shimeji mushrooms, bases trimmed and divided into small clusters
  or 4 oz (100 g) mushrooms of your choice, cut into bite-size pieces
3 slices cooked ham cut into ⅓-in (1-cm) strips **or** 3 small Vienna sausages *or* 1 frankfurter (cut into thin diagonal slices) *or* 3 slices bacon (cut into ⅓-in / 1-cm strips)
Additional butter, to taste

A ingredients—mix together:
1½ tablespoons soy sauce
1 tablespoon sugar
¾ tablespoon butter

1. Bring plenty of water to a boil in a pan, cook the udon noodles according to the package instructions, and drain into a colander.
2. Heat up the oil in a skillet over medium heat, and stir-fry the onion and mushrooms. When they are wilted add the ham and stir-fry quickly. Add the udon noodles and the A ingredients and stir-fry quickly.
3. Arrange on serving plates and top with additional butter.

Extra

This is delicious topped with mayonnaise to finish!

Ramen with Bacon & Lettuce

The key to the tastiness of this dish is to cook the bacon until it's crispy.

2 SERVINGS

2 servings fresh uncooked **Chinese noodles (thick type)** *or* 3 bundles dried somen noodles

3 oz (75 g) slab of bacon, cut into ¼-in (6-mm) strips

2 iceberg lettuce leaves (2 oz / 50 g), cut into 2-in (5-cm) pieces and torn *or* 2 loose-leaf lettuce leaves, torn *or* ½ small cucumber, sliced thinly

1 soft boiled egg, cut in half *or* ½ tomato, cut into wedges

Grated hard cheese, to taste

Coarse freshly ground black pepper, to taste

A ingredients—mix together:

2 tablespoons soy sauce

2 tablespoons fresh lemon juice

2 tablespoons water

1 tablespoon sugar

1 tablespoon olive oil

1. Bring plenty of water to a boil in a pan and boil the Chinese noodles according to the package instructions. Drain into a colander, rinse with cold running water, and drain well.

2. Put the bacon in a skillet over medium heat, and cook until it is crispy.

3. Arrange the Chinese noodles on serving plates, and top with the lettuce, bacon and boiled egg. Pour the combined A ingredients over, and sprinkle with grated cheese and coarsely ground black pepper.

NOTE: To make a soft boiled egg, add a room temperature egg to cold water to cover in a pan and bring up to a boil, lower the heat to medium-low and simmer for about 7 minutes.

Extra

Try sprinkling on some grated cheese or coarsely ground black pepper at the end, or add an extra pat of butter!

Soba with Sausage & Buttered Corn

Stir-frying Japanese soba noodles in the style of Chinese noodles is delicious too!

2 SERVINGS

2 servings frozen soba noodles
  or 2 servings ramen noodles
1 tablespoon butter
4 small Vienna sausages, cut into small pieces or 1 frankfurter (sliced) *or* 4 slices bacon (cut into ⅓-in / 1-cm strips) *or* 4 slices ham (cut into ⅓-in / 1-cm strips)
1 small can whole corn kernels (4 oz / 100 g), drained well or 4 green asparagus stalks, sliced thinly diagonally
Minced green onion (scallion), to taste

A ingredients—mix together:
1½ tablespoons soy sauce
1 tablespoon mirin
Pinch of salt

1. Bring plenty of water to a boil in a pan and cook the soba noodles according to the package instructions. Drain into a colander, rinse with cold running water, and drain well. If using ramen noodles instead, warm them up in a microwave oven and stir to separate the noodles.
2. Melt the butter in a skillet over medium heat, add the sausage and corn, and stir-fry until lightly browned. Add the soba noodles and the A ingredients, and stir-fry together quickly.
3. Arrange on serving plates, and sprinkle with minced green onion.

Lemony Noodles with Mackerel, Natto & Sliced Peppers

This noodle dish is packed with distinctive-tasting, nutritious ingredients. But the lemon soy sauce gives it all a refreshing taste. The thinly sliced raw shishito peppers provide a great flavor accent.

2 SERVINGS

3 bundles (5 oz / 150 g) dried somen noodles **or** 2 servings fresh Chinese noodles (thick type)

1 can mackerel packed in water (7 oz / 200 g), well drained and flaked roughly **or** ½ make-ahead steamed chicken (see page 10), shredded *or* 1 can tuna packed in water (5 oz / 150 g), well drained and flaked roughly

2 packets *natto* (fermented soy beans) with sauce (3 oz / 75 g)

8 shishito peppers, sliced thinly **or** 4 okra, sliced thinly *or* 1½ oz (40 g) *moroheiya* (Egyptian *mulukhiyah*) leaves, blanched and chopped

Lemon wedges, for serving

A ingredients:
1½ tablespoons soy sauce
1 tablespoon fresh lemon juice

Extra

You can add la-yu chili oil at the end to heighten the flavors, or add some torn-up nori seaweed as a topping!

1. Bring plenty of water to a boil in a pan and cook the somen noodles according to the package instructions. Drain into a colander, rinse with cold running water, and drain well.

2. Arrange the somen noodles on serving plates, top with the mackerel, *natto* and shishito peppers and pour the combined A ingredients over. Serve with lemon wedges.

Extra
Try adding roasted white sesame seeds or la-yu chili oil at the end!

Ramen with Mackerel, Garlic Chives & Kimchi

The sauce, which is made with fresh garlic chives, is a perfect match with the noodles.

2 SERVINGS

2 servings fresh uncooked ramen noodles (thick type) **or** 3 bundles dried somen noodles

1 can mackerel packed in water (7 oz / 200 g), well drained and flaked roughly **or** 4 oz (100 g) thinly sliced pork for shabu shabu, boiled

½ bundle garlic chives (about 2 oz (50 g), cut into ⅕-in (5-mm) pieces

2 heaping tablespoons napa cabbage kimchi, cut up roughly

A ingredients—mix together:
1½ tablespoons soy sauce
1 tablespoon sesame oil
½ tablespoon sugar

1. Bring plenty of water to a boil in a pan and boil the Chinese noodles according to the package instructions. Drain into a colander, rinse with cold running water, and drain well.
2. Put the A ingredients in a bowl and mix well. Add the chopped garlic chives, mix, and leave to steep for 2 to 3 minutes.
3. Arrange the Chinese noodles on serving plates, top with the mackerel and kimchi, and pour on the step-2 sauce.

Extra

Try adding shredded ginger, green shiso leaves or Asian leeks at step 2!

Soba with Tuna & Aromatic Greens

This is an ultra-easy, refreshing and delicious dish to make, where the only heat used is for cooking the noodles.

2 SERVINGS

2 servings frozen soba noodles **or** 2 servings frozen udon noodles *or* 3 bundles dried somen noodles

½ can / 1 small can (about 3 oz / 75 g) tuna packed in oil, drained **or** ½ make-ahead steamed chicken (see page 10), shredded *or* ½ can / 1 small can (about 3 oz / 75 g) mackerel (drained)

2 oz (50 g) *shungiku* (chrysanthemum greens)— tear off the leaves and cut the big ones in half. Slice the stems thinly diagonally **or** 2 oz (50 g) pea shoots, cut in half

2 *myoga* (Japanese ginger buds), cut in half lengthwise, and then thinly sliced crosswise

A ingredients—mix together:
2 tablespoons soy sauce
2 tablespoons sesame oil
One ½-in (1.25-cm) piece fresh ginger, peeled and grated

1. Bring plenty of water to a boil in a pan and cook the soba noodles according to the package instructions. Drain into a colander, rinse with cold running water, and drain well.

2. Put the A ingredients in a bowl and mix together. Add the soba, tuna, *shungiku* and *myoga* ginger buds, and mix well.

NOTE: I have used a 10-in (25-cm) diameter skillet. Arrange the ramen noodles in the skillet so that they overlap as little as possible.

Ramen with Tuna, Snow Peas & Shio Kombu

Once you have arranged all the ingredients in a skillet, all you need to do is cover it with a lid and steam-cook it! The cooking and clean-up are both easy. The *shio kombu* brings the flavors together.

2 SERVINGS

2 servings ramen noodles
2 oz (50 g) snow peas, strings removed
   or 3 green asparagus stalks, sliced thinly diagonally *or* 2 oz (50 g) garlic chives, cut into 2-in (5-cm) pieces
½ can or 1 small can (about 2½ oz / 65 g) tuna packed in oil, drained or ½ make-ahead steamed chicken (see page 10), shredded
⅓ oz *shio kombu* (salted kombu seaweed)
1 tablespoon roasted sesame seeds

A ingredients—mix together:
4 tablespoons water
1 tablespoon soy sauce
1 tablespoon mirin

Extra

This is also delicious topped with some bonito flakes or shredded nori seaweed!

1. Spread out the ramen noodles in a skillet, and top with the snow peas, tuna and *shio kombu*, in that order. Swirl in the A ingredients, cover with a lid, and steam-cook over high heat for about 4 minutes.
2. Take the lid off, add the sesame seeds and stir-fry quickly.

Try drizzling with la-yu chili oil!

Ramen with Shirasu, Tomato & Egg

Shirasu or *shirasuboshi* is salted whitebait. The creamy eggs and the cooked, softened tomatoes go together so well!

2 SERVINGS

3 eggs, beaten
1 oz (20 g) *shirasu* (whitebait)
or 1 oz (30 g) imitation crab sticks, shredded *or* 1 oz (30 g) canned tuna, drained
10 cherry tomatoes, cut into half lengthwise or
1 medium tomato, cut into wedges
1½ tablespoons oil, divided
2 servings thin ramen noodles, heated up in the microwave according to the package instructions and separated
Fresh coriander leaves (cilantro), chopped, to taste

A ingredients—mix together:
Pinch of salt
Freshly ground black pepper, to taste

B ingredients—mix together:
1½ tablespoons soy sauce
1½ tablespoons saké
½ tablespoon sugar
Pinch of salt
Freshly ground black pepper, to taste

1. Put the beaten eggs, *shirasu*, cherry tomato and A ingredients in a bowl and mix.
2. Heat up 1 tablespoon of the oil in a skillet over high heat, pour in the step-1 ingredients, and stir-fry while mixing in large circles. When the egg mixture is soft set, remove it from the pan.
3. Add the remaining ½ tablespoon of oil to the skillet over medium heat, and quickly stir-fry the ramen noodles and the B ingredients. Add the step-2 ingredients back in and stir-fry together quickly.
4. Arrange on serving plates and top with fresh coriander leaves.

The flavors really come together if you add coarsely ground black pepper to finish!

Ramen with Shredded Crab Stick & Egg

The shredded crab stick blends well with the noodles for even more deliciousness!

2 SERVINGS

2 servings fresh uncooked ramen (thick type) **or** ➡
3 bundles dried somen noodles **or** 2 servings frozen udon noodles
3 eggs, beaten
4 oz (100 g) imitation crab sticks, lightly shredded **or** ➡
½ make-ahead steamed chicken (see page 10), shredded **or** ½ can / 1 small can (about 3 oz / 75 g) tuna packed in oil, drained
2 tablespoons oil

A ingredients—mix together:
Pinch of salt
Freshly ground black pepper, to taste

B ingredients—mix together:
1 cup (250 ml) water
1 teaspoon Chinese chicken soup stock granules
2½ tablespoons soy sauce
1½ tablespoons rice vinegar
1½ tablespoons sugar
Dash of sesame oil

1. Bring plenty of water to a boil in a pan and boil the Chinese noodles according to the package instructions. Drain into a colander, rinse with cold running water, and drain well.
2. Put the eggs, imitation crab stick and A ingredients in a bowl and mix.
3. Heat up the oil in a skillet over high heat, add the step-2 ingredients and stir in large circles until the eggs are soft set.
4. Arrange the Chinese noodles on serving plates, and top with the step-3 ingredients. Pour the B ingredients into separate bowls and serve with the noodles. The noodles are dipped in the sauce to eat.

Tomato Salsa Somen

Once you have done the prep work, all you need to do is mix everything together! This Spanish-style tomato sauce is refreshing and delicious, and goes well with somen noodles. Try squeezing on some lemon for a refreshing finish.

2 SERVINGS

3 bundles (5 oz / 150 g) dried somen noodles
  2 servings fresh Chinese noodles (thick type)
2 tomatoes (10 oz / 330 g), cut into ⅓-in (1-cm) cubes
Fresh basil leaves, to taste (optional)

A ingredients:
3 tablespoons olive oil
1½ tablespoons soy sauce
1 tablespoon grated onion
1 teaspoon fresh lemon juice
¼ teaspoon salt
Freshly ground black pepper, to taste

Extra

This is delicious with a sprinkle of coarsely ground black pepper, or an extra squeeze of lemon to finish!

1. Bring plenty of water to a boil in a pan and cook the somen noodles according to the package instructions. Drain into a colander, rinse with cold running water, and drain well.
2. Put the A ingredients in a bowl and mix. Add the cubed tomato and mix well, then add the somen noodles and mix again.
3. Arrange on serving plates and top with basil leaves, if using.

Soba Topped with Mushrooms, Mountain Yam & Furikake

Add lots of red shiso leaf furikake for a fragrant finish.

2 SERVINGS

1 bag *nameko* mushrooms (about 4 oz / 100 g) *or*➤ 4 fresh okra pods (boiled and sliced) *or* 2 oz (50 g) *moroheiya* (Egyptian *mulukhiyah*) leaves, blanched and chopped

2 servings frozen soba noodles *or*➤ 2 servings frozen udon noodles *or* 3 bundles dried somen noodles

7 oz (200 g) mountain yam *or*➤ sweet potato, grated

1 heaping teaspoon red shiso furikake *or*➤ 2 *umeboshi*, pitted and chopped

Aonori seaweed powder, to taste

A ingredients—mix together:
1¼ cups (300 ml) chilled dashi stock
2 tablespoons soy sauce
½ teaspoon sugar
¼ teaspoon salt

1. Bring plenty of water to a boil in a pan, boil the *nameko* mushrooms for about a minute. Scoop them out with a slotted spoon and drain. With the water still boiling, cook the soba noodles according to the package instructions. Drain into a colander, rinse with cold running water, and drain well.
2. Arrange the soba noodles in serving bowls and top with the grated mountain yam and *nameko* mushrooms. Pour on the A ingredients and top with the red shiso furikake and *aonori* seaweed powder.

Extra

Great topped with *aonori* seaweed powder too!

Preserved Plum, Natto & Tofu Soba

This dish is packed with vegetable-based proteins! The *umeboshi* gives a refreshing taste.

2 SERVINGS

2 servings frozen soba noodles
 or 2 servings frozen udon noodles

1 small block (7 oz / 200 g) silken tofu **or** 7 oz (200 g) grated mountain yam

2 packets *natto* (fermented soy beans) with sauce (3 oz / 75 g)

2 *umeboshi* (1 oz / 30 g)

A ingredients—mix together:
1¼ cups (300 ml) chilled dashi stock
1½ tablespoons soy sauce
½ teaspoon sugar
½ teaspoon salt

1. Bring plenty of water to a boil in a pan, and cook the soba noodles according to the package instructions. Drain into a colander, rinse with cold running water, and drain well.
2. Put the tofu and *natto* in a bowl, and mix well while breaking up the tofu.
3. Arrange the soba noodles in bowls, and top with the step-2 ingredients. Pour on the A ingredients, and top with an *umeboshi* each.

NOTE: Use *umeboshi* that has 15% or less salt content. Adjust the amount of salt used depending on how salty the *umeboshi* is.

Extra
Try topping with fresh mint leaves for a delicious finish!

Thai Style Noodle Soup with Chicken & Bean Sprouts

So easy! These are somen noodles with a different flavor from the usual.

2 SERVINGS

2 bundles (4 oz / 100 g) dried somen noodles **or** ▶
   2 servings frozen udon noodles *or* 2 servings fresh Chinese noodles (thin type)

4 oz (100 g) bean sprouts

½ make-ahead steamed chicken (see page 10), sliced thinly **or** ▶ 4 oz (100 g) thinly sliced pork or beef for shabu shabu, boiled

¼ red onion, thinly sliced **or** ▶
   ¼ white onion, thinly sliced

Fresh coriander leaves (cilantro), chopped, to taste

Lime wedges, for serving

A ingredients:

3 cups (750 ml) water

½ tablespoon Chinese chicken soup stock granules

2½ tablespoon *nam pla* Thai fish sauce)

Pinch of salt

1. Bring plenty of water to a boil in a pan and cook the somen noodles according to the package instructions. Drain into a colander, rinse with cold running water, and drain well.

2. Put the A ingredients in a separate pan and mix. Bring to a boil over high heat, add the bean sprouts and boil for 30 seconds. Add the somen noodles and heat through.

3. Arrange the somen noodles in serving bowls, and top with the steamed chicken, red onion and coriander leaves. Serve with lime wedges.

Extra

This is delicious topped with thinly sliced make-ahead steamed chicken (page 10) too!

Nam Pla

It is a fish sauce similar to soy sauce that is made by fermenting salted fish for about a year. It is well liked in Japan. It has different levels of saltiness depending on the brand, so taste it and adjust the amounts used.

Noodle Soup with Coriander & Lemon

This somen dish has a delicious refreshing taste that is totally different from the usual salty-sweet flavor that results from using *mentsuyu* soup base!

2 SERVINGS

3 bundles (5 oz / 150 g) dried somen noodles **or** 2 servings fresh Chinese noodles (thick type)

Leaves of 2 small sprigs fresh coriander leaves (cilantro), cut into ⅓-in (1-cm) pieces

Lemon slices cut in half, for serving

A ingredients:
1¼ cups (300 ml) water
½ tablespoon Chinese chicken soup stock granules

2 tablespoon *nam pla* Thai fish sauce
1 small red chili pepper, sliced thinly

1. Bring plenty of water to a boil in a pan and cook the somen noodles according to the package instructions. Drain into a colander, rinse with cold running water, and drain well.
2. Put the A ingredients in a bowl and mix together. Add the chopped fresh coriander leaves and mix.
3. Arrange the somen noodles in bowls, and top with lemon slices. Put the step-2 sauce in separate bowls, and serve with the noodles.

Extra
This is also delicious sprinkled with thinly sliced red chili pepper!

Ramen with Ground Meat, Green Onions & Fish Sauce

Even if the ingredients are familiar, simply using fish sauce to flavor the meat distinguishes this dish from the usual fare in a remarkable way.

2 SERVINGS

2 servings ramen noodles
5 oz (150 g) ground pork **or**
   5 oz (150 g) ground chicken,
   mixed with 2 tablespoons
   nam pla Thai fish sauce, 1
   teaspoon sugar, a pinch
   of salt and coarse freshly
   ground black pepper, to taste
4 tablespoons water
5 thin green onions (scallions),
   cut into 2-in (5-cm) pieces
   or ½ Asian leek, cut into 2-in
   (5-cm) pieces and sliced thinly
   or ½ bundle garlic chives
   (about 2 oz / 50 g), cut into
   2-in (5-cm) pieces
Coarsely chopped peanuts, to
   taste

1. Spread out the ramen noodles in a skillet. Distribute the ground meat on top of the noodles. Swirl in the water, cover the pan with a lid, and steam-cook over high heat for about 4 minutes.
2. Take off the lid and stir-fry for about 1 minute. When all the meat has changed color, add the green onion and stir-fry quickly.
3. Arrange on serving plates and sprinkle with the chopped peanuts.

NOTE: I recommend using a 10-in (25-cm) diameter skillet. Arrange the ramen noodles in the skillet so that they overlap as little as possible.

Extra

Try adding some roughly chopped fresh coriander leaves (cilantro)!

Thin Ramen with Shrimp & Egg

I created this dish with the iconic pad Thai stir-fried noodles as the inspiration.

2 SERVINGS

1½ tablespoons oil, divided
3 eggs, beaten and mixed with a pinch of salt and freshly ground black pepper, to taste
5 oz (150 g) peeled and cleaned shrimp (devein, if necessary) **or** 5 oz (150 g) mixed seafood
¼ onion, thinly sliced **or** 4 oz (100 g) bean sprouts
2 servings ramen noodles, warmed in the microwave according to the package instructions **or** 3 bundles dried somen noodles, cooked
Coarse freshly ground black pepper

A ingredients—mix together:
1½ tablespoons *nam pla* Thai fish sauce
½ tablespoon soy sauce
½ tablespoon sugar
Pinch of salt
Freshly ground black pepper, to taste

1. Heat up 1 tablespoon of the oil over high heat in a skillet. Pour in the beaten egg mixture, and mix in a large circular motion as you stir-fry. When the egg mixture is soft set, remove it from the pan.
2. Add the remaining ½ tablespoon of the oil to the skillet and heat over medium heat. Add the shrimp and onion and stir-fry. When the shrimp changes color, add the ramen noodles and the A ingredients, and stir-fry together. Add the step-1 egg mixture back in and stir-fry quickly.
3. Arrange on serving plates and sprinkle with coarsely ground black pepper.

SAVORY SALTED NOODLES

Ramen with Pea Shoots & Pork

Namul is a Korean side dish of seasoned par-boiled vegetables. Simply using salt, pepper and sesame oil creates lots of flavor! Adding citrus juice at the end balances out the taste. You can vary the ingredients in this dish in several ways, so it's a handy recipe to have in your repertoire.

2 SERVINGS

4 oz (100 g) thinly sliced pork for shabu shabu `or` ½ make-ahead steamed chicken (see page 10), shredded *or* 2 chicken tenderloins, cooked and shredded

2 servings fresh Chinese noodles (thick type) `or` 2 servings frozen udon noodles *or* 3 bundles dried somen noodles

2 oz (50 g) pea shoots, roots trimmed `or` 2 oz (50 g) *mizuna* greens, cut into 1½-in (3.75-cm) pieces *or* 4 oz (100 g) bean sprouts, roots trimmed

Sliced lime, for serving

A ingredients:
2 tablespoons sesame oil
1 teaspoon salt
Coarse freshly ground black pepper, to taste

Extra

Delicious with some grated garlic or ginger added at step 2 too!

1. Bring plenty of water to a boil in a pan. Add the pork and boil over low heat. When it changes color, take it out with a slotted spoon, drain, and leave to cool. Raise the heat to high and boil the Chinese noodles according to the package instructions. Thirty seconds before the noodles are done, add the pea shoots. Drain them both into a colander, rinse with cold running water, and drain well.

2. Put the A ingredients in a bowl and mix. Add the step-1 ingredients and mix.

3. Arrange on serving plates and top with lime slices. Squeeze on the lime to eat.

Extra

This is tasty when topped with some grated daikon radish too!

Udon with Pork & Sliced Citrus

Sudachi is a green citrus fruit that is used in Japan in the same way as lemon or lime. It adds a refreshing taste to this delicious dish, which is perfect when the weather is hot.

2 SERVINGS

4 oz (100 g) thinly sliced pork for shabu shabu **or** ½ make-ahead steamed chicken (see page 10), sliced thinly

2 servings frozen udon noodles **or** 3 bundles dried somen noodles *or* 2 servings fresh Chinese noodles (thick type)

2 *sudachi* **or** 1 small lime, sliced thinly

A ingredients—mix together:
1¼ cups (300 ml) water
⅓ teaspoon Chinese chicken soup stock granules
1 teaspoon salt
⅓ teaspoon soy sauce

1. Bring plenty of water to a boil in a pan. Add the pork and boil over low heat. When it changes color, take it out with a slotted spoon, drain, and leave to cool. Raise the heat to high and boil the udon noodles according to the package instructions. Drain into a colander, rinse with cold running water, and drain well.

2. Arrange the noodles in serving bowls, top with the pork and *sudachi* slices, and pour over the combined A ingredients.

Extra
Try adding some minced garlic or ginger at step 1—delicious!

Thin Ramen with Pork & Cucumber

Stir-fried cucumber increases in sweetness and goes well with noodles and pork.

2 SERVINGS

Meat-rub paste mixture consisting of 1 tablespoon saké, a pinch of salt and 1 teaspoon potato starch or cornstarch
5 oz (150 g) roughly chopped pork **or** 5 oz (150 g) ground pork
2 servings ramen noodles
2 small (or 1 large) cucumbers, cut in half lengthwise and sliced thinly **or** 1 zucchini, cut in half lengthwise and sliced thinly *or* 3 cabbage leaves, shredded
1 red chili pepper, deseeded
3 tablespoons water

A ingredients:
1 tablespoon sesame oil
1 teaspoon salt

1. Prepare the meat-rub paste mixture and apply it to the pork.
2. Spread the ramen noodles out in a skillet, and spread out the cucumber, pork and red chili pepper on top, in that order. Swirl in the water, cover with a lid, and steam-cook for about 4 minutes over high heat.
3. Take off the lid and add the A ingredients. Stir-fry for about a minute until all the meat changes color.

NOTE: I recommend using a 10-in (25-cm) diameter skillet. Arrange the ramen noodles in the skillet so that they overlap as little as possible.

Chicken Noodle Soup with Lettuce

Nyumen is the Japanese word for hot somen noodles. When lettuce is cooked and becomes wilted, you can eat a lot of it! This dish is appetizing in hot or cold weather. This meal makes for a great excuse to eat somen noodles at any time!

2 SERVINGS

2 bundles (4 oz / 100 g) dried somen noodles or 2 servings frozen udon noodles

½ make-ahead steamed chicken (see page 10), skin removed and shredded into bite-size pieces or 4 oz (100 g) thinly sliced pork for shabu shabu, boiled

⅓ head iceberg lettuce (about 4 oz / 100 g), torn into large pieces or 6 oz (175 g) *komatsuna* greens, cut into 1½-in (3.75-cm) pieces *or* 2 cabbage leaves, torn

Sesame oil, to taste

A ingredients:
3 cups (750 ml) water
½ tablespoon Chinese chicken soup stock granules
Pinch of salt

Extra

If you add coarsely ground black pepper at the end, the flavors will really come together!

1. Put the A ingredients in a pan and mix. Bring to a boil over high heat, add the somen noodles and the steamed chicken, and cook over medium heat for about 1 minute 30 seconds.
2. Add the lettuce, boil quickly, and swirl in some sesame oil.

NOTE: The somen noodles are cooked in the broth without boiling them first. Somen noodles already have salt in them, so you only need to add a little extra salt.

Ramen with Chicken, Celery & Olive Oil

A generous amount of olive oil really brings out the fragrance and flavor of raw celery. Combine with low-calorie chicken tenderloins for a healthy dish.

2 SERVINGS

2 chicken tenderloins (about 4 oz / 100 g), tendons removed **or** ½ make-ahead steamed chicken (see page 10), shredded

2 servings fresh Chinese noodles (thick type) **or** 3 bundles dried somen noodles

½ large celery stalk, tough strings removed and sliced thinly diagonally **or** 2 oz (50 g) *mizuna* greens, cut into 1½-in (3.75-cm) pieces *or* 2 oz (50 g) baby greens

A ingredients:
½ tablespoon saké
Pinch of salt

B ingredients:
2 tablespoons olive oil
¾ teaspoon salt

1. Place the chicken tenderloins on a microwave-safe dish and sprinkle with the A ingredients. Cover loosely with cling wrap and cook in the microwave for about 1 minute, 40 seconds. Leave with the cling wrap on to continue cooking with residual heat. When the chicken has cooked sufficiently, shred up the chicken tenderloins into bite-size pieces.
2. Bring plenty of water to a boil, and cook the Chinese noodles according to the package instructions. Drain into a colander, rinse with cold running water, and drain well.
3. Put the B ingredients in a bowl and mix. Add the Chinese noodles, chicken and celery, and mix well.

Extra

Try adding grated cheese to finish, or serving with lemon wedges!

Spicy Dan Dan Somen

A somen noodle dish with punchy Sichuan-style flavors. It really perks you up!

2 SERVINGS

1 teaspoon oil
1 teaspoon doubanjiang
½ **clove garlic, minced** *or* one
  ½-in (1.25-cm) piece fresh
  ginger, peeled and minced
5 oz (150 g) **ground pork** *or*
  5 oz (150 g) ground beef *or*
  5 oz (150 g) coarsely chopped
  pork
½ **tablespoon soy sauce**
3 bundles (5 oz / 150 g) dried
  somen noodles
Fresh coriander leaves
  (cilantro), roughly chopped,
  to taste
La-yu chili oil, to taste

A ingredients—mix together:
1¼ cups (300 ml) soy milk
1 teaspoon soy sauce
⅔ teaspoon salt

1. Add the oil, doubanjiang and
garlic to a skillet over medium
heat, and stir until fragrant. Add
the ground pork and stir-fry.
When the meat changes color,
stir in the soy sauce.
2. Bring plenty of water to
a boil in a pan, and cook the
somen noodles according to
the package instructions. Drain
into a colander, rinse with cold
running water, and drain well.
3. Arrange the somen noodles
in serving bowls, top with the
step-1 ingredients and pour the
combined A ingredients over
top. Add the coriander leaves
and la-yu chili oil.

Extra

Add some lemon juice at the end for a refreshing flavor kick!

Thin Ramen with Ground Pork & Lettuce

The key to this dish is to just barely cook the lettuce so that it retains its crispness.

2 SERVINGS

½ tablespoon sesame oil

½ clove garlic, sliced thinly

½ red chili pepper, deseeded and sliced thinly

5 oz (150 g) ground pork
or 5 oz (150 g) coarsely chopped pork, **mixed with 1 tablespoon saké, a pinch of salt and 1 teaspoon potato starch or cornstarch**

½ head iceberg lettuce (about 5 oz / 150 g), torn into bite-size pieces **or** 7 oz (200 g) *komatsuna* greens, cut into 1½-in (3.75-cm) pieces **or** 3 cabbage leaves, torn up

2 servings ramen noodles, warmed up in the microwave and separated according to the package instructions **or** 2 servings frozen udon noodles, cooked **or** 3 bundles dried somen noodles, cooked

¾ teaspoon salt

1. Add the sesame oil, garlic and red chili pepper to a skillet over medium heat, and stir until fragrant. Add the ground meat and stir-fry.

2. When the ground meat changes color, add the lettuce and stir-fry quickly. Add the ramen noodles and salt, and stir-fry together.

Carbonara Style Udon with Mushrooms & Bacon

If you make carbonara with udon noodles instead of traditional pasta, it becomes surprisingly light-tasting and has a pleasing aftertaste.

2 SERVINGS

2 servings frozen udon noodles
½ tablespoon oil
4 oz (100 g) shimeji mushrooms, bases trimmed and divided into small clusters **or** 4 oz (100 g) mushrooms of your choice, cut into bite-size pieces *or* 6 oz (175 g) *komatsuna* greens, cut into 1½-in (3.75-cm) pieces
2 slices bacon, cut into ⅓-in (1-cm) strips **or** 2 Vienna sausages, sliced thinly diagonally *or* 1 frankfurter, sliced thinly diagonally
Coarse freshly ground black pepper, to taste

A ingredients—mix together:
2 eggs
⅖ cup (100 ml) milk
3 tablespoons grated hard cheese
½ teaspoon salt
Grated garlic, to taste

1. Bring plenty of water to a boil in a pan, cook the udon noodles according to the package instructions, and drain into a colander.
2. Heat up the oil in a skillet over medium heat, and stir-fry the mushrooms. When they are wilted, add the bacon and stir-fry quickly. Add the udon noodles and the combined A ingredients, and mix together quickly.
3. Arrange on serving plates, and sprinkle with coarsely ground black pepper.

> **NOTE:** The key is to turn off the heat and mix quickly once the egg mixture has been added to the pan so that it does not cook too much. I call for regular whole cow's milk. If you use low-fat or skim milk, the flavor will be lighter.

Extra

Try adding some torn-up green shiso leaves at the end!

Somen with Bacon & Eggplant

This version of *champuru*, a traditional Okinawan dish, is richly flavored because of the bacon, so you only need to add a small amount of seasoning.

2 SERVINGS

3 bundles (5 oz / 150 g) dried somen noodles **or** 2 servings frozen udon noodles

2½ tablespoons olive oil, divided

1 clove garlic, sliced thinly

2 small Asian eggplants, cut into 6 pieces lengthwise, and then each piece cut in half diagonally **or** 1 small zucchini, cut into half lengthwise and sliced thinly, *or* 4 small (or 1 large) bell peppers, sliced thinly

4 slices bacon, cut into ½-in (1.25-cm) pieces **or** 4 Vienna sausages, cut thinly diagonally, *or* 2 frankfurters, cut thinly diagonally, *or* ½ can or 1 small can (about 2½ oz / 65 g) tuna packed in oil, drained

A ingredients—mix together:
¾ teaspoon salt
Dash of soy sauce

1. Bring plenty of water to a boil in a pan, and cook the somen noodles according to the package instructions. Drain into a colander, rinse with cold running water, and drain well. Mix the noodles with ½ table-spoon of the olive oil.
2. Add remaining 2 table-spoons of the olive oil and the garlic to a skillet over medium heat, and stir until fragrant. Add the eggplant and stir-fry. When the eggplant has wilted, add the bacon and stir-fry.
3. Add the somen noodles and the A ingredients to the pan, and stir-fry quickly.

Extra

Adding thinly sliced onion or whole corn kernels at step 1 is delicious too!

Noodle Soup with Sausage & Cabbage

This dish is similar to an Italian pasta soup.

2 SERVINGS

4 Vienna sausages, sliced thinly diagonally or➤ 2 frankfurters, sliced thinly diagonally, *or* 4 slices bacon, cut into ⅓-in (1-cm) pieces, *or* 1 small can (about 2½ oz / 65 g) tuna packed in oil, drained

2 large cabbage leaves (about 4 oz / 100 g), cut into bite-size pieces or➤ 4 oz (100 g) spinach, cut into 1½-in (3.75-cm) pieces, *or* 2 large lettuce leaves, cut into bite-size pieces

2 bundles (4 oz / 100 g) dried somen noodles or➤ 2 servings frozen udon noodles

Grated hard cheese, to taste

A ingredients:
3 cups (750 ml) water
½ tablespoon consommé granules
Pinch of salt
Freshly ground black pepper, to taste

1. Put the A ingredients in a pan and mix. Bring to a boil over high heat, add the sausage and cabbage and cook over medium heat for 2 to 3 minutes.
2. When the cabbage has wilted, add the somen noodles and cook for about a minute.
3. Ladle into serving bowls and sprinkle with grated cheese.

NOTE: The somen noodles are cooked in the broth without boiling them first. Somen noodles already have salt in them, so you only need to add a little extra salt.

Udon with Crisp Greens, Tarako Butter & Nori

Tarako is salted pollock roe, which is packed with umami. It is available fresh or frozen at Japanese grocery stores. Richly flavored *tarako* butter is combined with the crispness of raw *mizuna* greens for a refreshing contrast in textures. This goes well with somen noodles too.

2 SERVINGS

2 servings frozen udon noodles **or**
  3 bundles dried somen noodles
1 piece *tarako* **(about 2 oz / 50 g), membrane removed and the eggs scraped out of the sac** **or** 1 piece
  mentaiko (spicy pollock roe)
2 oz (50 g) *mizuna* **greens** **or** Spinach
  leaves **cut into 1½-in (3.75-cm) pieces**
Shredded nori seaweed, to taste

A ingredients:
1 tablespoon butter
Pinch of salt

Extra

> Try adding some minced green onions (scallions), Asian leek or radish sprouts together with the *mizuna* greens!

1. Bring plenty of water to a boil in a pan, cook the udon noodles according to the package instructions, and drain into a colander.
2. Put the udon noodles, *tarako* and A ingredients in a bowl and mix together vigorously until the butter has melted. Add the *mizuna* greens and mix quickly.
3. Arrange on serving plates and sprinkle with shredded nori seaweed.

Extra

This is delicious with shredded Asian leek, radish sprouts and natto (with the sauce) added too!

Soba with Tuna, Wakame, Ginger & Sesame

The ginger in this dish really whets the appetite! The tuna and sesame oil lend rich flavor.

2 SERVINGS

2 servings frozen soba noodles **or** 2 servings frozen udon noodles *or* 3 bundles dried soba noodles

½ can or 1 small can (about 2½ oz / 65 g) tuna packed in oil, drained **or** 4 oz (100 g) canned mackerel in water, drained

¹⁄₁₀ oz (3 g) or a large pinch of dried, cut-up wakame seaweed, rehydrated in water for about 5 minutes and squeezed out

Roasted white sesame seeds, to taste

A ingredients:
2 tablespoons sesame oil
¾ teaspoon salt
One ½-in (1.25-cm) piece fresh ginger, peeled and grated

1. Bring plenty of water to a boil in a pan, boil the soba noodles according to the package instructions, and drain into a colander. Rinse with cold running water, and drain well.
2. Put the A ingredients in a bowl and mix. Add the soba noodles, tuna and wakame seaweed and mix.
3. Arrange on serving plates and sprinkle with roasted sesame seeds.

Great topped with a fried egg too!

Soba Peperoncino with Dried Fish & Greens

Chirimen jako are small salted dried fish similar to *shirasu* (page 42), but drier. The unexpected combination of *chirimen jako* and *komatsuna* greens makes for a delicious dish!

2 SERVINGS

2 servings frozen soba noodles
or 2 serving frozen udon noodles *or* 3 bundles dried soba noodles
2 tablespoons olive oil
2 cloves garlic, minced

1 red chili pepper, deseeded and sliced thinly
½ oz (15 g) *chirimen jako* (dried young sardines) **or** 2 Vienna sausages, sliced thinly diagonally *or* 1 frankfurter, sliced thinly diagonally
4 oz (100 g) *komatsuna* greens, cut into 1-in (3-cm) pieces
or 4 oz (100 g) spinach, cut into 1-in (2.5-cm) pieces
⅔ teaspoon salt

1. Bring plenty of water to a boil in a pan, and boil the soba noodles according to the package instructions. Take out ¼ cup (70 ml) of the cooking water while the noodles are cooking and reserve. Drain the noodles into a colander, rinse with cold running water, and drain well.
2. Heat the olive oil, garlic and red chili pepper in a skillet over low heat. When it is fragrant, add the *chirimen jako* and *komatsuna* greens, and stir-fry over medium heat.
3. When the *komatsuna* greens are wilted, add the soba, the reserved soba cooking water and salt, and mix quickly.

Extra

Try adding shredded cucumber or daikon radish for a delicious variation!

Ramen with Crab Sticks, Radish Sprouts & Lemony Dipping Sauce

The refreshingly delicious salty lemon dipping sauce goes with all kinds of dishes.

2 SERVINGS

2 servings fresh Chinese noodles (thick type) or 3 bundles dried somen noodles

3½ oz (85 g) imitation crab sticks, roughly shredded or ½ can or 1 small can (about 2½ oz / 65 g) tuna packed in oil, drained *or* 4 oz (100 g) canned mackerel in water, drained

¼ oz (10 g) radish sprouts, roots trimmed or ¼ onion, thinly sliced

A ingredients—mix together:
1¼ cups (300 ml) water
1 teaspoon Chinese chicken soup stock granules
1 tablespoon fresh lemon juice
⅔ teaspoon salt
½ teaspoon sugar

1. Bring plenty of water to a boil, and cook the Chinese noodles according to the package instructions. Drain into a colander, rinse with cold running water, and drain well.

2. Arrange the Chinese noodles on serving plates, and top with the crab sticks and radish sprouts. Put the combined A ingredients in separate serving bowls and serve with the noodles. Dip the noodles and other ingredients into the sauce to eat.

Extra

Sprinkle on *shichim togarashi* (seven-ingredient chili pepper mix) to finish for a delicious variation!

Yuzu Udon Soup with Fish Cake & Greens

This hot udon has a comforting flavor. It's a dish you'll want to eat when yuzu is in season.

2 SERVINGS

4 oz (100 g) *komatsuna* greens
or 4 oz (100 g) spinach
2 servings frozen udon noodles
or 2 bundles dried somen noodles
1½-in (3.75-cm) piece *kamaboko* fish cake, cut into ⅓-in (1-cm) slices **or** 1 *chikuwa* fish stick, cut thinly diagonally
Shredded yuzu peel **or** Meyer lemon peel, **to taste**

A ingredients—mix together:
3 cups (750 ml) dashi stock
2 tablespoons mirin
1¼ teaspoons salt
½ teaspoon soy sauce

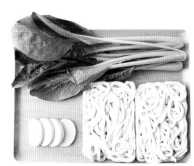

1. Bring plenty of water to a boil in a pan. Add the *komatsuna* greens and blanch quickly. Take the greens out with a slotted spoon and place in cold water to cool. Drain and squeeze out, and cut into 1½-inch (4-cm) pieces. Bring the water in the pan back to a boil and cook the udon noodles according to the package instructions. Drain into a colander.

2. Add the mixed A ingredients to a separate pan, and bring to a boil over high heat.

3. Arrange the udon noodles in serving bowls, ladle in the step-2 soup, and top with *kamaboko* fish cake, the *komatsuna* greens and yuzu peel.

Ramen with Gazpacho Dipping Sauce

A refreshing Spanish gazpacho-style sauce with grated onion and cucumber is used here as a noodle dipping sauce. Despite its festive appearance, it is made by simply mixing the ingredients—it's amazingly easy to make!

2 SERVINGS

2 servings fresh Chinese noodles (**thick type**) **or** 3 bundles dried somen noodles

½ **small (or ¼ large) cucumber or** ¼ zucchini, **cut into ¼-in (6-mm) cubes**

A ingredients—mix together:
2 eggs
1⅔ **cups (400 ml) tomato juice (no salt-added)**
2 **tablespoons olive oil**
1 **tablespoon fresh lemon juice**
1¼ **teaspoons salt**
1 **teaspoon grated onion**

Extra

Delicious served with hot sauce too!

1. Bring plenty of water to a boil, and cook the Chinese noodles according to the package instructions. Drain into a colander, rinse with cold running water, and drain well.

2. Arrange the Chinese noodles on serving plates. Pour the combined A ingredients in separate bowls, top with the cucumber and serve with the noodles. Dip the noodles in the sauce to eat.

NOTE: I recommend using chilled tomato juice.

Korean Style Chilled Ramen

This is an easy-to-make version of the Korean noodle dish, *kong-guksu* (noodles in soy milk soup)! The kimchi really does the heavy lifting here.

2 SERVINGS

2 servings fresh Chinese noodles (thick type) **or** 3 bundles dried somen noodles

4 oz (100 g) napa cabbage kimchi, chopped

½ small (or ¼ large) cucumber, cut into 2-in (5-cm) long thin matchsticks **or** 1 oz (30 g) radish sprouts, roots trimmed or ¼ zucchini, cut into 2-in (5-cm) long thin matchsticks

1 soft boiled egg, cut in half **or** 2 hot-spring poached eggs (see page 14)

Roasted sesame seeds, to taste

A ingredients—mix together:

1⅔ cups (400 ml) soy milk

1 teaspoon salt

1. Bring plenty of water to a boil in a pan and cook the Chinese noodles according to the package instructions. Drain into a colander, rinse with cold running water, and drain well.

2. Arrange the Chinese noodles in serving bowls, and pour over the combined A ingredients. Top with the kimchi, cucumber and boiled egg, and sprinkle with roasted sesame seeds.

NOTE: To make a soft boiled egg, add a room temperature egg to enough cold water to cover in a pan and bring up to a boil. Then, lower the heat and cook over medium-low heat for about 7 minutes.

Extra

Try adding shredded make-ahead steamed chicken (page 10) at step 2, or doubanjiang for added spice!

Sesame Sauce Ramen with Tofu & Salted Mustard Greens

Takana (*haam choy*) is pickled Japanese mustard greens, and it has a salty, pungent flavor. It adds great flavor to this dish! This is a healthy stir-fry dish with tofu as the main ingredient.

2 SERVINGS

1 tablespoon sesame oil

1 small block (about 7 oz / 200 g) firm tofu, torn into large pieces and wrapped in paper towels to drain off the water **or** 1 small block (about 7 oz / 200 g) silken tofu, drained well

4 oz (100 g) *takana* pickles **or** kimchi, **chopped**

2 servings ramen noodles, warmed in the microwave according to the package instructions and separated **or** 2 servings frozen udon noodles, cooked

1½ tablespoons roasted white sesame seeds

⅓ teaspoon salt

1. Heat up the sesame oil in a skillet over medium heat. Add the tofu and *takana* green pickles, and stir-fry while breaking up the tofu.

2. When the tofu is lightly browned and crumbled, add the ramen noodles, roasted sesame seeds and salt, and stir-fry quickly.

Extra

This is also delicious topped with minced green onions, grated fresh ginger, roasted white sesame seeds or fresh lemon juice!

Taiwan Style Mixed Ramen

Re-create this popular Taiwanese noodle dish easily! Mix well before eating.

2 SERVINGS

2 servings fresh ramen (thin type) **or** 2 servings frozen udon noodles

½ tablespoon oil

7 oz (200 g) ground pork **or** 7 oz (200 g) ground beef

½ bundle garlic chives (about 2 oz (50 g), chopped into ⅕-in (5-mm) pieces, with root ends removed

Bonito flakes, to taste

Shredded nori seaweed, to taste

2 fresh or pasteurized raw egg yolks **or** 2 hot-spring poached eggs (see page 14)

A ingredients—mix together:

2 tablespoons saké

1 tablespoon oyster sauce

½ teaspoon soy sauce

Grated garlic, to taste

NOTE: Because the garlic chives are eaten raw, be sure to trim off the thick root ends.

1. Bring plenty of water to a boil in a pan and cook the Chinese noodles according to the package instructions. Drain into a colander, rinse with cold running water, and drain well.

2. Heat the oil in a skillet over medium heat, and stir-fry the ground meat while crumbling it finely. When the meat changes color, add the combined A ingredients, and stir-fry until everything is combined.

3. Arrange the Chinese noodles on serving plates, top with the step-2 ingredients, garlic chives, bonito flakes, shredded nori seaweed and raw egg yolks. Mix up to eat.

Oyster Sauce

This is a distinctly Chinese seasoning sauce that is often used in stir-fries. It goes well with noodles; not only does it have umami, but it adds depth and distinction to the flavor of the dish.

Extra

At step 1, try adding thinly diagonally sliced Asian leek or thinly sliced onion, or adding doubanjiang to the A ingredients to make the sauce spicy!

Udon with Oyster Dipping Sauce

The hearty, rich dipping sauce is quite a departure from the usual with this type of dish.

2 SERVINGS

5 oz (150 g) boneless chicken thigh, cut into bite-size pieces **or** 5 oz (150 g) thinly sliced pork belly, cut into 1-in (2.5-cm) pieces

3 shiitake mushrooms, stems removed and sliced thinly **or** 2 oz (50 g) mushrooms of your choice, cut into bite-size pieces **or** 2 oz (50 g) bean sprouts

2 servings frozen udon noodles **or** 2 servings frozen soba noodles **or** 3 bundles dried somen noodles

Coarsely ground chili pepper, to taste

A ingredients—mix together:
1¼ cups (300 ml) water
1 teaspoon Chinese chicken soup stock granules
2 tablespoons oyster sauce
1 teaspoon soy sauce
½ teaspoon sugar

1. Mix the A ingredients in a pan, and bring to a boil over high heat. Add the chicken and shiitake mushrooms, and simmer over medium-low heat for about 3 minutes.
2. Bring plenty of water to a boil in a separate pan, cook the udon noodles according to the package instructions, and drain into a colander. Rinse with cold running water, and drain well.
3. Arrange the udon noodles on serving plates. Put the step-1 sauce into separate bowls, sprinkle with coarsely ground chili pepper, and serve with the udon noodles. Dip the noodles in the sauce to eat.

Extra

Try adding grated garlic and / or ginger to the A ingredients!

Shanghai Style Ramen with Shrimp & Cucumber

Cooked cucumber and oyster sauce go so well together!

2 SERVINGS

2 servings ramen noodles

2 small (or 1 large) cucumbers, cut into quarters lengthwise, and then cut into 2-in (5-cm) pieces **or** 4 oz (100 g) pea shoots (cut in half)

5 oz (150 g) peeled shrimp (deveined, if necessary) **or** 5 oz (150 g) ground pork *or* 5 oz (150 g) ground chicken

4 tablespoons water

Coarse freshly ground black pepper, to taste

Lemon wedges, for serving

A ingredients—mix together:

1½ tablespoons oyster sauce

1 tablespoon soy sauce

1 tablespoon saké

I recommend using a 10-in (25-cm) diameter skillet. Arrange the ramen noodles in the skillet so that they overlap as little as possible.

1. Spread out the ramen noodles in a skillet, and place the cucumber and shrimp on top in that order. Swirl in the water and then the combined A ingredients, cover the pan with a lid, and steam-cook over high heat for about 4 minutes.

2. Remove the lid, and stir-fry until all the shrimp change color, about 1 minute.

3. Arrange on serving plates and sprinkle with coarsely ground black pepper. Serve with lemon wedges, and squeeze the juice on before eating.

Ginger & Oyster Sauce Ramen with Dried Shrimp, Bean Sprouts & Garlic Chives

Sakura shrimp or *sakura-ebi* are tiny dried shrimp available at Japanese grocery stores. They add a nice accent to the deep flavors.

2 SERVINGS

2 servings ramen noodles
7 oz (200 g) bean sprouts **or** ½ onion, thinly sliced *or* 1 Asian leek, thinly sliced diagonally
¼ bundle (about 1 oz / 30 g) garlic chives, cut into 2-in (5-cm) pieces **or** 5 thin green onions (scallions), cut into 2-in (5-cm) pieces
3 tablespoons sakura shrimp
4 tablespoons water

A ingredients—mix together:
2 tablespoons oyster sauce
1 tablespoon saké
½ tablespoon soy sauce
One ½-in (1.25-cm) piece fresh ginger, peeled and minced

1. Spread out the ramen noodles in a skillet, and place the bean sprouts, garlic chives and sakura shrimp on top, in that order. Swirl in the water and then the combined A ingredients, cover with a lid, and steam-cook for about 4 minutes over high heat.
2. Remove the lid, and stir-fry until all the ingredients are incorporated.

MISO FLAVORED NOODLES

Extra

Try sprinkling on coarsely ground chili pepper at the end!

Miso Udon with Pork & Eggplant

Pork, eggplant and miso is a combination that can't be beat! By using the miso to pre-flavor the meat, the dish will not be too heavily flavored and will have a light finish. Bamboo shoots work well in this dish too.

2 SERVINGS

2 servings frozen udon noodles or 3 bundles dried somen noodles

Meat-rub paste mixture consisting of 2 tablespoons each miso and mirin

5 oz (150 g) chopped pork, 2 tablespoons

2 Asian eggplants, cut into half lengthwise, and then cut into ⅓-in (1-cm) pieces or 5 oz (150 g) boiled or canned bamboo shoot, sliced thinly *or* 1 small can whole corn kernels (4 oz / 100 g), drained

2 tablespoons oil

2 tablespoons water

Green shiso leaves, to taste

Roasted white sesame seeds, to taste

1. Bring plenty of water to a boil in a pan, cook the udon noodles according to the package instructions, and drain into a colander.

2. Prepare the meat-rub paste mixture and apply it to the pork.

3. Put the eggplant and oil in a skillet and mix. Spread out in the skillet, and top with the pork. Sprinkle with water, cover with a lid, and steam-cook for about 4 minutes over medium heat. Take the lid off, add the udon noodles and stir-fry.

4. Arrange on serving plates, tear up some shiso leaves and distribute on top, and sprinkle with roasted white sesame seeds.

Extra

Add some dried anchovies (*niboshi*) to the A ingredients for a delicious twist!

Pork & Cabbage Udon with Miso Sauce

The subtly spicy dipping sauce is addictive. You'll never get tired of this noodle dish!

2 SERVINGS

2 cabbage leaves, about 4 oz (100 g) **or** 3–4 lettuce leaves *or* 1 small bok choy, **cut into bite-size pieces**

4 oz (100 g) **thinly sliced pork shoulder for shabu shabu or** make-ahead steamed chicken (see page 10), thinly sliced

2 **servings frozen udon noodles or** 3 bundles dried somen noodles

Grated garlic, to taste

A ingredients—mix together:
1 **cup (250 ml) water**
1 **teaspoon Chinese chicken soup stock granules**
1½ **tablespoons miso**
1 **tablespoon ground sesame seeds**
½ **teaspoon soy sauce**
½ **teaspoon doubanjiang**

1. Bring plenty of water to a boil in a pan, and add the cabbage leaves, and then the pork, and boil them briefly over low heat. Take out with a slotted spoon and cool in a colander. Return the heat to high and boil the udon noodles according to the package instructions. Drain into a separate colander, rinse with cold running water, and drain well.

2. Combine the A ingredients in another pan, and bring to a boil over high heat.

3. Arrange the udon noodles on plates, and top with the cabbage, pork and a little grated garlic. Ladle the step-2 ingredients into separate bowls and serve with the noodles. Dip the noodles in the sauce to eat.

Miso Udon Soup with Pork Belly & Leek

The generous amount of leeks will warm you up from the inside.

2 SERVINGS

4 oz (100 g) thinly sliced pork belly, cut into 2-in (5-cm) pieces **or** 4 oz (100 g) coarsely chopped pork *or* 4 oz (100 g) coarsely chopped beef

1 Asian leek, sliced diagonally into ⅕-in (5-mm) slices, including the green tops **or** ½ onion, thinly sliced

2 servings frozen udon noodles **or** 2 bundles dried somen noodles, boiled

Coarsely ground chili pepper, to taste

A ingredients:
3⅓ cups (800 ml) dashi stock
3 tablespoons miso

Note: In this recipe, the frozen udon noodles are cooked as-is in the soup.

1. Put the A ingredients in a pan and mix. Bring to a boil over high heat, add the pork and leek, and simmer over medium heat for 1 to 2 minutes. When the pork changes color, add the udon noodles, and simmer for another 3 minutes or so.

2. Put into serving bowls, and sprinkle with coarsely ground chili pepper.

Spicy Zhajiang Noodles

This take on the classic Chinese noodles adds lots of vegetables to the well-flavored meat sauce to make it healthier. You don't even need a knife to prep the vegetables. You can make this dish in no time.

2 SERVINGS

2 servings fresh Chinese noodles (thick type)
> *or* 2 servings frozen udon noodles

1 teaspoon sesame oil
½ teaspoon doubanjiang
5 oz (150 g) ground pork
1 small (or ½ large) cucumber, struck with a rolling pin to fracture it all over, and broken into bite-size pieces
> *or* 1 small tomato, cut into wedges

2 loose-leaf lettuce leaves, about 1½ oz (40 g), torn into bite-size pieces *or* 1–2 iceberg lettuce leaves, torn into bite-size pieces
Mayonnaise, for serving

A ingredients—mix together:
2 tablespoons miso
2 tablespoons water
½ tablespoon soy sauce
½ tablespoon sugar
Pinch of potato starch or cornstarch

Extra

> Try adding a hot-spring poached egg (page 14) at the end, or sprinkling with roasted white sesame seeds!

1. Bring plenty of water to a boil in a pan and cook the Chinese noodles according to the package instructions. Drain into a colander, rinse with cold running water, and drain well.
2. Put the sesame oil and doubanjiang in a skillet over medium heat. When the oil is fragrant, add the ground meat and stir-fry. When the meat has changed color, add the combined A ingredients, and stir-fry until the sauce is a little thickened.
3. Arrange the Chinese noodles on serving plates, top with the step-2 sauce, cucumber and lettuce, and serve with a dollop of mayonnaise on the side.

Chilled Summer Udon Soup with Mackerel & Miso

Hiyajiru is a traditional Japanese dish that is usually made with cold rice. This version with udon noodles is topped with lots of aromatic summer vegetables for a refreshing, delicious flavor! The soup, which is lightly flavored with miso, brings everything gently together.

2 SERVINGS

2 servings frozen udon noodles 2 servings frozen soba noodles *or* 3 bundles dried somen noodles
One 7-oz (200-g) can mackerel packed in water one 5-oz (150-g) can tuna packed in water, **well drained and flaked roughly**
1 small (or ½ large) cucumber ½ zucchini, **sliced thinly, sprinkled with salt, rested for 5 minutes, and then squeezed out well**
2 *myoga* Japanese ginger buds, sliced thinly into rounds
5 green shiso leaves, shredded
Ground sesame seeds, to taste

A ingredients—mix together:
⅖ cup (100 ml) ice water
1½ tablespoons miso
½ tablespoon soy sauce
1 teaspoon sugar

Extra
Delicious with shredded ginger added at the end too!

1. Bring plenty of water to a boil in a pan, cook the udon noodles according to the package instructions, and drain into a colander.
2. Arrange the udon noodles in serving bowls, top with the mackerel, cucumber, *myoga* ginger and green shiso leaves, pour the combined A ingredients over top and sprinkle with the ground sesame seeds.

Extra

This is delicious with thinly sliced onion or thinly sliced diagonally Asian leek stir-fried with the spinach too!

Sesame Miso Noodles with Spinach

This delicious miso-flavored take on the Okinawan classic is quite different from the usual *champuru*!

2 SERVINGS

3 bundles (5 oz / 150 g) dried somen noodles **or** 2 servings frozen udon noodles

1 teaspoon sesame oil

½ tablespoon oil

5 oz (150 g) spinach, cut into 2-in (5-cm) pieces **or** 4 oz (100 g) bean sprouts *or* 5 oz (150 g) *komatsuna* greens, cut into 2-in (5-cm) pieces

3 *chikuwa* fish sticks (3½ oz / 85 g), cut in half lengthwise, and then sliced into ⅕-in (5-mm) wide pieces **or** ½ can or 1 small can (about 2½ oz / 65 g) tuna packed in oil, drained

A ingredients—mix together:

1½ tablespoons miso

1½ tablespoons mirin

1 tablespoon soy sauce

1 tablespoon ground sesame seeds

1. Bring plenty of water to a boil in a pan, and cook the somen noodles according to the package instructions. Drain into a colander, rinse with cold running water, and drain well. Mix the noodles with the sesame oil.

2. Heat up the oil in a skillet over medium heat, and stir-fry the spinach. When it is wilted, add the *chikuwa* fish sticks and stir-fry together. Add the somen noodles and the combined A ingredients, and stir-fry quickly.

Extra

Add *beni-shoga* (red pickled ginger) at the end for a tasty twist!

Miso Ramen with Bean Sprouts & Fried Egg

This is an unusual miso-flavored stir-fry dish with easy-to-cook ingredients.

2 SERVINGS

2 teaspoons oil, divided
2 eggs
Salt and coarse freshly ground
  black pepper, to taste
7 oz (200 g) bean sprouts
  or 4 oz (100 g) pea shoots,
  cut in half
2 servings ramen noodles,
  warmed in the microwave
  according to the package
  instructions and spread out
  or 2 servings frozen udon
  noodles
Aonori seaweed powder,
  to taste

A ingredients:
2 tablespoons miso
2 tablespoons mirin
½ tablespoon soy sauce
Pinch of coarse freshly ground
  black pepper

1. Heat up 1 teaspoon of the oil in a skillet over medium-high heat. Break in the eggs, sprinkle in salt and coarsely ground black pepper, and then fry the eggs to your desired degree of doneness. Remove the eggs from the skillet.
2. Heat up the remaining teaspoon of the oil in the same skillet after removing the eggs and heat over high heat. Stir-fry the bean sprouts. When they are wilted, add the ramen noodles and the combined A ingredients and stir-fry together quickly.
3. Arrange on serving plates, top with the fried eggs and sprinkle with *aonori* seaweed powder.

Cold Somen with Shredded Cucumber and Soy Milk Dipping Sauce

Plenty of cucumber makes this a beautiful looking somen dish!

2 SERVINGS

3 bundles (5 oz / 150 g) dried somen noodles **or** 2 servings fresh Chinese noodles (thick type)

2 small (or 1 large) cucumber **or** 1 zucchini, shredded very thinly with a vegetable slicer

Roasted white sesame seeds, to taste

A ingredients—mix together:
1¼ cups (300 ml) soy milk
2 tablespoons miso
¼ teaspoon salt

1. Bring plenty of water to a boil in a pan and cook the somen noodles according to the package instructions. Drain into a colander, rinse with cold running water, and drain well.

2. Mix the somen noodles and cucumber together and arrange on serving plates. Sprinkle on the roasted white sesame seeds. Serve the combined A ingredients as a sauce in separate bowls, and dip the noodles in the sauce to eat.

Extra
Try adding some coarsely ground chili pepper to finish!

Miso Noodle Soup with Napa Cabbage

This is a *nyumen* (hot somen) dish that warms you up on cold days.

2 SERVINGS

2 pieces *abura-age* (thin deep-fried tofu), cut in half lengthwise, and then cut into 1-in (2.5-cm) pieces **or** 2 *chikuwa* fish sticks cut thinly diagonally *or* 2 oz (50 g) *kamaboko* fish cake, cut into ⅓-in (1-cm) slices

2 napa cabbage leaves (about 5 oz / 150 g) **or** 3 cabbage leaves, **cut into bite-size pieces**

2 bundles (4 oz / 100 g) dried somen noodles **or** 2 servings frozen udon noodles

Minced thin green onion (scallion), to taste

A ingredients:
3⅓ cups (800 ml) dashi stock
1 tablespoon miso

1. Put the A ingredients in a pan and mix together. Bring to a boil over high heat and add the *abura-age* and napa cabbage. Simmer over medium heat for about 3 minutes. When the napa cabbage is wilted, add the somen noodles, and cook for about 1 minute, 30 seconds.
2. Put into serving bowls and top with minced green onions.

Note: The somen noodles are cooked in the broth without boiling them first. Somen noodles already have salt in them, so you only need to add a little extra salt.

Extra
Try adding thinly shaved burdock root or shredded ginger at step 1!

Soup Curry Somen with Pork & Eggplant

If you get bored with the usual soy-sauce-and-dashi-based somen sauce, try this! The curry flavor is addictive.

2 SERVINGS

3⅓ oz (100 g) chopped pork
  or 4 oz (100 g) thinly sliced pork belly, cut into 2-in (5-cm) pieces *or* 4 oz (100 g) chopped beef
1 Asian eggplant, cut into ⅓-in (1-cm) wide diagonal slices, and then cut into sticks **or** 1 Asian leek, sliced thinly diagonally *or* 4 oz (100 g) mushrooms of your choice, cut into bite-size pieces
3 bundles (5 oz / 150 g) dried somen noodles **or** 2 servings frozen udon noodles

A ingredients:
1¼ cups (300 ml) dashi stock
2 tablespoons soy sauce
2 tablespoons mirin
2 teaspoons curry powder

1. Combine the A ingredients in a pan and bring to a boil over high heat. Add the pork and eggplant, and simmer for about 2 minutes over medium heat.
2. Bring plenty of water to a boil in a separate pan and cook the somen noodles according to the package instructions. Drain into a colander, rinse with cold running water, and drain well.
3. Arrange the somen noodles on serving plates. Ladle the step-1 sauce into separate bowls, and serve with the noodles. Dip the noodles in the sauce to eat.

Curry Powder

Curry powder differs depending on the spices that are blended to make it, so choose the brand that you like. If you are making curry-flavored dishes for children, you can reduce the amounts.

Extra

Also delicious with grated garlic or ginger added to the A ingredients!

Somen with Beef & Mushrooms

This is a curry-flavored variation of the traditional Okinawan dish, *champuru*. It is very hearty.

2 SERVINGS

3 bundles (5 oz / 150 g) dried somen noodles **or** 2 servings frozen udon noodles

½ tablespoon sesame oil

1 teaspoon oil

5 oz (150 g) chopped beef, sprinkled with salt and freshly ground black pepper **or** 5 oz (150 g) thinly sliced pork belly, cut into 2-in (5-cm) pieces and sprinkled with salt and freshly ground black pepper

4 oz (100 g) maitake mushrooms, divided into easy-to-eat clumps **or** 4 oz (100 g) mushrooms of your choice, cut into bite-size pieces

¼ onion, thinly sliced **or** ½ Asian leek or 1 large green onion (scallion), thinly sliced diagonally

A ingredients—mix together:
2 tablespoons soy sauce
2 tablespoons saké
1 teaspoon curry powder

1. Bring plenty of water to a boil in a pan and cook the somen noodles according to the package instructions. Drain into a colander, rinse with cold running water, and drain well. Mix the noodles with the sesame oil.

2. Heat up the oil in a skillet over medium heat, and stir-fry the beef. When the meat changes color, add the maitake mushrooms and the onion and stir-fry together.

3. When the onion is wilted, add the somen noodles and the combined A ingredients, and stir-fry together.

Extra

Try adding minced ginger with the garlic, or topping the dish with hot-spring poached eggs (page 14)!

Tomato Curry Ramen

Both children and adults are sure to love these flavors. Stir-fried tomatoes are delicious!

2 SERVINGS

½ tablespoon oil
½ clove garlic, finely minced
7 oz (200 g) ground beef and pork **or** 7 oz (200 g) ground beef *or* 7 oz (200 g) chopped beef
1 tablespoon curry powder
2 small tomatoes (about 8 oz / 250 g), cut into 8 wedges
2 servings ramen noodles, heated up in the microwave according to the package instructions and separated

A ingredients:
¼ cup (65 ml) water
2 tablespoons tomato ketchup
1 tablespoon Japanese Worcestershire sauce or *tonkatsu* sauce
¼ teaspoon salt

1. Put the oil and garlic in a skillet over medium heat. When the oil is fragrant, add the meat and stir-fry, until the meat changes color. Add the curry powder and stir-fry until it is incorporated. Add the tomatoes and A ingredients and stir-fry together.
2. When everything is well blended and a little thickened, add the ramen noodles and stir-fry quickly.

Extra
Also delicious with shimeji or maitake mushrooms divided into clumps, or bean sprouts, simmered with the leek!

Curry Udon Soup with Fish Sticks & Leek

This udon dish tastes somehow nostalgic. Try thickening the soup at the end with potato starch or cornstarch dissolved in water.

2 SERVINGS

2 servings frozen udon noodles
or 2 bundles dried somen noodles

3 *chikuwa* fish sticks (3½ oz / 85 g), cut into ⅓-in (1-cm) wide diagonal slices **or** 4 oz (100 g) thinly sliced pork belly, cut into 2-in (5-cm) pieces *or* 4 oz (100 g) chopped pork

1 Asian leek (use the green tops too) **or** 1 large green onion (scallion), cut into ⅓-in (1-cm) wide diagonal slices

A ingredients—mix together:
3 cups (750 ml) dashi stock
3 tablespoons mirin
2½ tablespoons soy sauce
2 teaspoons curry powder
⅓ teaspoon salt

1. Bring plenty of water to a boil in a pan and cook the udon noodles according to the package instructions. Drain into a colander.

2. Mix the A ingredients together in a separate pan and bring to a boil over high heat. Add the *chikuwa* fish sticks and leek, and simmer for about 2 minutes over medium heat. Add the udon noodles and bring back to a boil.

"Books to Span the East and West"

Tuttle Publishing was founded in 1832 in the small New England town of Rutland, Vermont [USA]. Our core values remain as strong today as they were then—to publish best-in-class books which bring people together one page at a time. In 1948, we established a publishing outpost in Japan—and Tuttle is now a leader in publishing English-language books about the arts, languages and cultures of Asia. The world has become a much smaller place today and Asia's economic and cultural influence has grown. Yet the need for meaningful dialogue and information about this diverse region has never been greater. Over the past seven decades, Tuttle has published thousands of books on subjects ranging from martial arts and paper crafts to language learning and literature—and our talented authors, illustrators, designers and photographers have won many prestigious awards. We welcome you to explore the wealth of information available on Asia at **www.tuttlepublishing.com**.

Published by Tuttle Publishing, an imprint of Periplus Editions (HK) Ltd.

www.tuttlepublishing.com

ISBN 978-4-8053-1884-3

Kihon Chomiryou de Tsukuru 5 fun Men
Copyright © 2021 Etsuko Ichise
English translation rights arranged with
SHUFU-TO-SEIKATSUSHA, LTD.
through Japan UNI Agency, Inc., Tokyo

English translation © 2024 Periplus Editions (HK) Ltd
Translated from Japanese by Makiko Itoh

Printed in China   2410EP

28 27 26 25 24
10 9 8 7 6 5 4 3 2 1

TUTTLE PUBLISHING® is a registered trademark of Tuttle Publishing, a division of Periplus Editions (HK) Ltd.

Distributed by

North America, Latin America & Europe
Tuttle Publishing
364 Innovation Drive
North Clarendon
VT 05759-9436 U.S.A.
Tel: (802) 773-8930
Fax: (802) 773-6993
info@tuttlepublishing.com
www.tuttlepublishing.com

Japan
Tuttle Publishing
Yaekari Building 3rd Floor
5-4-12 Osaki Shinagawa-ku
Tokyo 141 0032
Tel: (81) 3 5437-0171
Fax: (81) 3 5437-0755
sales@tuttle.co.jp
www.tuttle.co.jp

Asia Pacific
Berkeley Books Pte. Ltd.
3 Kallang Sector, #04-01
Singapore 349278
Tel: (65) 6741-2178
Fax: (65) 6741-2179
inquiries@periplus.com.sg
www.tuttlepublishing.com